Gift of

The John W. Bowman Family

in memory of

TIMOTHY DILLON BOWMAN

REHEARSING THE REVOLUTION

Marie-Hélène Huet

Rehearsing the Revolution

THE STAGING OF MARAT'S DEATH
1793–1797

translated by
Robert Hurley

University of California Press

Berkeley   Los Angeles   London

University of California Press
Berkeley and Los Angeles, California
University of California Press, Ltd.
London, England
© 1982 by
The Regents of the University of California

LIBRARY OF CONGRESS CATALOGING
IN PUBLICATION DATA

Huet, Marie-Hélène.
Rehearsing the Revolution.
1. Marat, Jean Paul, 1743–1793, in fiction, drama,
poetry, etc.   2. French drama—18th century—
History and criticism.   I. Title.
PQ538.H8   842'.6'09351   81-21965
ISBN 0-520-04321-9   AACR2

Printed in the United States of America

1 2 3 4 5 6 7 8 9

Dans les maisons ouvertes, la
lie de la population immunisée,
semble-t-il par sa frénésie
cupide, entre et fait main basse
sur des richesses dont elle sent
bien qu'il est inutile de profiter.
Et c'est alors que le théâtre
s'installe. Le théâtre, c'est-à-dire
la gratuité immédiate qui pousse
à des actes inutiles et sans
profit pour l'actualité.

Les derniers vivants s'exaspèrent,
le fils, jusque-là soumis et
vertueux, tue son père.

Antonin Artaud

Contents

1

Louis XVI's Head, and Jean-Paul Marat's

January 16, 1793, at the theater of the Tuileries. The auditorium is packed; the representation about to unfold is the conclusion of a trial that has gone on just short of two months; today the Convention will decide in favor of the king's death. The voting procedure has still not been determined. On the threshold of this final act, various, seemingly trivial concerns are slowing down the proceedings. For instance, there is the question of *L'Ami des Lois,* Laya's *pièce à scandale.* Should the play be censored, or should it not? The discussion drags on. Danton loses patience and protests: "A comedy indeed! The matter before us is the tragedy you owe the nations; the thing at issue is the head of a tyrant which we are going to sever with the axe of the laws."[1] This tragedy is finally staged, and to the question "What penalty shall be inflicted?" the representatives of the people come, one by one, to the rostrum and answer in a voice loud enough to be heard by the entire audience. As we know, this performance lasted seventy-two hours, and on 17 January the Convention voted the death of Louis Capet, King of France and Father of the People.

The nineteenth century was to see that judicial action as a parricide, as the unthinkable crime the memory of which would bear heavily on the accursed children of the Revolu-

1. Quoted in Jules Michelet, *Histoire de la Révolution française,* 2 vols. (Paris: Bibliothèque de la Pléiade, 1952), 2:174.

tion. It should not be thought, however, that the ritual that decided the death of the Father was marked by the gravity that would seem appropriate to that irremediable event. In spite of the ineluctable, hence necessarily tragic, character of the performance, a festive atmosphere prevailed in the theater. This is how an eyewitness quoted by Michelet speaks of it: "No doubt you imagine a state of composure, a kind of awe-inspired silence in that auditorium. Not at all. The back of the hall was converted into loges in which ladies dressed with the most charming carelessness ate oranges or ices and drank liqueurs."[2] "The elegant, fashionable side," Michelet adds,

was the one containing the galleries near the Montagne. The great fortunes sat on that side of the Convention, under the protection of Marat and Robespierre. Orléans was there, and Lepelletier, and Hérault de Séchelles, and the Marquis de Chateauneuf, and Anarchazis Cloutz—many very rich men. Their mistresses came covered with tricolored ribbons, filling the reserved galleries.[3]

"The *huissiers* on the Montagne side," says Mercier,

played the part of opera loge attendants, gallantly showing ladies to their places. Although any sign of approbation was forbidden, on that side nonetheless the old Duchess, the Amazon of the Jacobin bands, uttered long cries of "Well! Well!" whenever she did not hear the word death ring out. The upper galleries, reserved for the people, were full of foreigners and spectators of every class, who drank wine and spirits as if it were a tavern. Boredom, impatience, and fatigue marked every face. Each deputy ascended in turn to the rostrum. You could hear them asking: "Is my turn coming up?" A sick deputy was called in; he came decked out in his nightcap and dressing gown. This phantom moved the Assembly to laughter. . . . To the rostrum came faces that were rendered more dismal by

2. Sébastien Mercier, quoted in Michelet, *Histoire de la Révolution française,* 2:171.
   3. Ibid., 2:172.

the pale gleam of the lights, as in a slow and sepulchral voice they uttered the one word, Death! All those physiognomies that followed one another in succession, all those different tones, those different gamuts; Orléans, who was hooted, jeered, when he declared for the death of his relative; and the others who calculated whether they would have time to eat before they gave their vote, while women pricked cards with pins to compare the votes; deputies who dropped off to sleep and had to be roused to vote.[4]

The women pricking their cards with pins, the stocking-knitters counting heads and their stitches to the clicking of their needles: the revolutionary legend was already taking form. Consider for a moment the image of that sick deputy in a dressing gown and nightcap, that specter whose garb could not fail to recall Rousseau and whose ludicrous form, about to decide the death of the king, gave rise to laughter and derision. Danton was not wrong to protest; this was not comedy but tragedy—although the public did not perceive it as such, for many more hours would have to pass before the 17 January session would take on in retrospect all the gravity the situation called for.

The witness's account underscores the fact that we are indeed within the register of the theater: the material organization, the public, the stage, the loges, the ushers, the galleries. The distribution of elements: that noisy, frivolous, enthusiastic theater-going crowd of which Diderot was so fond, and the more sober representatives of the people, loudly declaiming a sentence the repetitiveness of which brought out its force. The text was in dialogue form, as in the theater; however, in this instance the dialogue went beyond the theatrical and bore within it, amid the tumult and the levity of the auditorium, a force that was truly revolutionary. *Monarchy* spells *monologue:* "I, François, by the grace of God . . . . I, Louis, by the grace of God . . . ."—the grace and undisputed majesty in the first person that op-

4. Ibid.

pressed France for centuries. The absolutism of *je.* 1793: in that unthinkable trial, *tu* was obligatory, the *tu* of the classical tragedies rather than the ceremonious plural of the court. Dialogue: the *je* replies to the *tu;* it is the object of a question: "Citizen Ducos, what do you say? Death. Garrau—Death. Boyer-Fonfrède—Death. Duplantier—Death unconditional. Robespierre—Death. Collot d'Herbois—Death. Manuel—Confinement in a stronghold elsewhere than Paris, until the public interest shall permit deportation. Billaud-Varenne—Death within twenty-four hours. Camille-Desmoulins—Death. Marat—Death within twenty-four hours."[5] Danton was right: this was a tragedy, and never would the twenty-four hours of the unity of time acquire a more essentially tragic dimension; their application here could not have had a more serious justification. Time kills; you vote for death without delay. The people in the galleries were getting drunk and eating ices; it was the end of the first act.

This theater was not theater, of course; under the exterior signs of a frivolous scene almost familiar in its frightening levity, History was unfolding. That it borrowed the mask of comic illusion is not insignificant; that the quasi-grotesque paraded next to the tragic should not necessarily surprise us. But let us consider the text. Contrary to the theatrical text, this one was not written beforehand, although in a sense the script was known by all from the first day of the trial. Here what was declaimed aloud was written down almost immediately afterward. Present on the stage was a silent, quaint, forgotten personage, a figure of no importance who nevertheless could symbolize the new revolutionary order: the clerk. Even as the tragedy was enacted, he wrote it down. No sooner had he written it than the actor,

5. Albert Soboul, *Le Procès de Louis XVI* (Paris: Collection Archives Juillard, 1966), p. 214.

the people's representative, signed it. This putting into writing, solemn but discreet, effective and implicit, also bore witness to history.

The written declaration and the proclamation were the two sides of democratic thought. In fact, the Assembly passed no law that was not immediately the subject of a public proclamation:

> As soon as the present law has come before the constituted authorities, they shall read it aloud in their public sessions during three consecutive days, and shall cause it to be posted and proclaimed to the beating of the drum, so that no one may pretend ignorance of it.[6]

The written object must be proclaimed and, conversely, the proclaimed object must be put in writing, thus attesting the Assembly's constant concern for the legitimacy of its acts. The written formulation was the order of the law; it was the definitive, irremediable inscription of revolutionary thought. This was the site where the modest and unceasing work of the innumerable clerks—those anonymous and indispensable artisans of the Revolution's judicial edifice—was carried out.

The condemnation of Louis XVI: a theatrical manifestation nearly perfect despite its length; tragedy and comedy, a lively audience, serious or ridiculous actors, but a reversal of the relation of text to proclamation. It was not the theatrical text that was represented, it was the representation that became a text, that is, a sentence. Danton had declared with his customary force: "Kings are struck only at the head."[7] *Frapper,* "to strike," as in "to strike coins": "I will pay you back in your own coin, and you will treat yourselves to the king's head." For that matter, the louis was no longer in

6. Session of 26 July 1793, *Le Moniteur,* no. 210.
7. Soboul, *Le Procès de Louis XVI,* p. 219.

circulation. The Bourbon profile had ceased to be legal currency; what with the *assignat* and inflation, paper was king. The sentence was written and the king's head would fall. Witness the trial report and the decree that was adopted, which reads as follows:

Article I. The National Convention declares Louis Capet, last king of the French people, guilty of conspiring against the public liberty, and of attacks upon the general security of the state.

Article II. The National Convention decrees that Louis Capet shall suffer the death penalty.

Article III. The National Convention declares null the writ of Louis Capet, brought before the bar by his counselors, called "Appeal to the Nation against the Judgment Rendered against Him by the Convention," and forbids anyone to act upon it, under penalty of pursuit and punishment as one guilty of treason against the Republic.

Article IV. The Provisional Executive Council shall this day notify Louis Capet of the present decree, and shall take the police and security measures necessary to ensure its implementation within twenty-four hours from the time of notification, and shall give a full report to the National Convention immediately after it has been implemented.[8]

As early as 1789, the Criminal Jurisprudence Committee had insisted on the public character of the work of justice. Thus Baumetz had asked for and obtained the opening of judicial proceedings to the people:

Admit the public to the reading of the depositions, to the confrontation of witnesses who have given evidence before the warrant . . . admit the public to the findings of the additional inquiry, and to the ensuing confrontations. . . . But the act that demands, above all others, to be made public, the one that must complete the tranquillity of innocence and win for the magistrates a tribute of merit, confidence, and esteem, is the report of the trial.[9]

8. Ibid., p.224.
9. *Le Moniteur,* October 1789, no. 65.

As we see here, the public factor was not, in the eyes of the legislator, simply a demagogic tactic. It constituted one of the safeguards of justice, the protection of innocence. The semi-theatrical organization of the trial that unfolds in front of an informed audience, from whom nothing is concealed, ensured the integrity of the proceedings and sufficed to protect the accused from a mundane anxiety: judicial error. In this context, silence was associated with the deviation or deformation of the juridical process: the public proclamation, the staging of justice, was at the basis of the very operation of the law. Two new elements therefore come into focus. (1) The importance of the word is that of the law. When the jurors declared their verdict aloud, when the witnesses delivered their deposition audibly, and when, finally, the sentence became the object of a declamation, it was revolutionary justice that was being practiced. (2) The writing came after the spoken word. That the *mise en page* was done after the oral, public proclamation, that the clerk, the writer, took his place after the reciter—this too was in the revolutionary order of things. The judicial system established by the National Constituent Assembly was conceived as a kind of anti–*lettre de cachet,* the symbol of a monarchic justice in which the letter, the written order, interned, expelled, banished, and executed, all in the velvet silence of absolutism. The *lettre de cachet* was the sealed, concealed, discreet, secret, powerful and irreversible order; its antithesis and antidote were the public proclamation and the transcription of that proclamation, which in turn would be distributed and read aloud. *Le Moniteur,* the most important newspaper of the Revolution, was an oddity in the history of the daily paper. It gave a day-to-day account of the deliberations of the Assembly in all their monotony, their pusillanimity, their gravity, their inconstancy. It did not classify, analyze, or delete. Nothing was so trivial that it should be suppressed: everything that was said must be printed, and everything printed must be proclaimed.

Even silence and absence became an object of publication.

Thus Rouger and Jean Bon Saint-André demanded that the people's representatives absent on 16 and 17 January 1793 be put on a list and officially reprimanded and that their names be communicated to the departments.

The trial was so long and tumultuous that the execution was, by contrast, striking for its swiftness and austerity. Though it was public, a large empty space separated the condemned man from the crowd, and troops presented a formidable barrier between Louis and his people: "It was ten minutes after ten when he arrived in the square. Standing under the columns of the Admiralty were the *commissaires* of the Commune, there to draft a report of the execution. A large empty space, ringed with cannons, had been reserved around the scaffold; beyond, as far as the eye could reach, one saw troops. Consequently, the spectators were extremely far away."[10]

In the great judicial movement that was to withdraw the body of the criminal from the public gaze, the execution of Louis XVI already marked a symbolic difference worth reflecting upon. Doubtless the royal body was not, could not be, the criminal body. The Assembly, and Robespierre, had sensed that a royal judgment was not possible; one might say that it was Louis Capet who was thus offered to the curiosity of Parisians on the day of his execution, and that it was the king of France who was separated from his people by that immense vacant space and by the massive deployment of military forces. The end of a cycle—Louis XVI, King of France, was executed, but the death of the Father was simultaneously the constituting of an inheritance; the fallen father left a vacancy over which the parricidal sons would quarrel. What was this inheritance, for that matter, if not an uneasy straddling between remembrance— the deceased father—and anticipation—the successor; a transmission of powers without a transmitter, an obsession

10. Michelet, *Histoire de la Révolution française,* 2:187.

with a genealogy which, as the whole Revolution vigorously affirmed, had just come to an end. In the judgment,
Louis Capet was called the *last* king of France; in the bill of
public indictment, the Father of the People was simultaneously stripped of his lineage and his paternity; yet, even
before the king's execution, Louvet shouted to Danton,
who had taken the floor without asking the chairman: "You
are not yet king, Danton!"[11]

Closer to the people, hence closer to the question of filiation, was Jean-Paul Marat. In those first months of the year
1793, the People's Friend had lost some of his virulence:
witness this curious episode mentioned in the *Mémoires* of
Barras.

> One day Marat saw some poor devil of a *ci-devant,* all dressed in
> black, walking along the rue Saint-Honoré being pursued by a
> rabble. Luckily Marat happened to be passing by and saved the
> man in a most original way: "I know him," said Marat, "I know the
> aristocrat." (He had never seen him.) "There, that'll teach you," he
> added, giving him a kick in the behind. Everyone laughed. The
> crowd drifted away convinced that as the kings of old cured scrof-
> ula by the royal touch, so the People's Friend cured the aristocracy
> by a well-placed boot.[12]

The irony was cruel; the sick Marat curing the *ci-devant,*
Marat the former doctor who was unable to rid himself of
his own infirmity, compared to the king he had condemned
and from whom he took a curative power he had not been
able to receive as an inheritance—this too was in the symbolic order of the Revolution.

Marat as a distinctive individual was in fact completely
obliterated by history in favor of a systematization, an exalted mystification. Michelet gives evidence of this phe-

11. Ibid., p. 175.
12. *Mémoires de Barras,* cited by Jules Michelet, *History of the French
Revolution,* vols. 4, 6, and 7, trans. Keith Botsford (Wynnewood, Pa.:
Livingston Publishing Company, 1973), 6:136.

nomenon: "In public imprecations, perhaps for the sake of the rhyme, anyway in the most childish fashion—which reveals the depth, the blind frivolity of local passion—the names of Marat and Garat are paired."[13] The Revolution operated as well, perhaps primarily, in the order of language. Names were so many signs having the force of law, from the nobiliary particle to the democratic *tutoiement,* but proper names were not neutral. Take the name Robespierre: *la robe,* the magistrature inscribed on the cold countenance of the lawyer from Arras; *la pierre,* the very core of the Incorruptible. *Robe/pierre, robe-ès-pierre;* does not the passionate interest of posterity in that discreet figure have as its touchstone the configuration of a name so heavy to bear? Thus the People's Friend, their parricidal protector, became symbolically more vulnerable when the king's death left a vacancy. It was an irony of history that the moment he "became human," in Michelet's words, he was assassinated. In that month of July, Marat was overcome with fatigue, "he too looked as though he were wearing down somewhat," says Furet.[14] His death was to complete a cycle. Michelet writes concerning Louis XVI's sepulcher: "A closed tomb wants silence, but this one is not closed, it is open wide and asking."[15] In a sense, the death of Marat was to be the gravestone of Louis XVI.

In Charlotte Corday's scheme the symbolic element was uppermost: she intended to strike Marat on 14 July, the anniversary of the fall of the royalty, and she would strike him where his greatest crime had been committed, in that very theater where Marat had demanded the death of Louis XVI within twenty-four hours. Marat's illness spoiled her plan: he died at home, the evening of 13 July, more as a sick person than as a criminal. With Marat stabbed, Charlotte

13. Michelet, *History of the French Revolution,* 6:127.

14. François Furet and Denis Richet, *La Révolution française* (Paris: Fayard, 1973), p. 189.

15. Michelet, *Histoire de la Révolution française,* 2:189.

Corday accepted her own death sentence with no apparent regret. Concerned about the head that was going to fall in public—once again—she had a bonnet made for her during her captivity. It took some time for the newspapers to learn to spell the name Charlotte Corday correctly, for she was an unknown. Thus Marat's assassination did not have the public, theatrical character she had hoped for. It would be the theater that would instead, by presenting on the stage the idealized death of the revolutionary, restore all the force of the murder and the sacrifice.

The last segment of our introduction: a half-dozen successful plays inspired by the death of Jean-Paul Marat were performed between 1793 and 1797. One put the assassination back where it ought to have taken place, on the stage of the National Convention, while another staged the opening of the assassin's trial; nearly all of them, in the apotheosis that concludes most revolutionary plays, brought the People's Friend back to life, returning, surrounded by various figures representing Liberty, Justice, Equality, to remain forever the counselor and inspiration of the Republic. Louis XVI's tomb was now firmly closed, Marat's was wide open. *L'Ami du Peuple, ou la mort de Marat* (*The People's Friend, or the Death of Marat*), by Gassier Saint Amand, was presented less than a month after the deputy's death, on 8 August 1793, at the Théâtre des Variétés Amusantes; *Marat dans le souterrain, ou la journée du 10 août* (*Marat in the Caves, or the Day of 10 August*), by Mathelin, opened in December at the Théâtre de l'Opéra-Comique National; *La Mort de Marat,* by Citizen Barrau, was presented in February 1794. After Thermidor, Marat's assassination continued to inspire dramatists, and with three plays glorifying Charlotte Corday the revolutionary legend was established.

Thus a series of elements or events in history or in the revolutionary legend forms a communication network one terminal of which is the theatrical representation of Marat's death:

At the two extremes (1 and 6) of the network above,
are Louis XVI's trial and the theatrical representation of
Marat's death; these two stations, apparently incongruous
in nature if one sticks to an analysis of history and illusion,
actually comprise many identical elements or functions. To
begin with, there is the theatrical aspect, evident in the session at the theater of the Tuileries in the course of which
Louis was condemned before a general audience; and, at the
Variétés or the Opéra-Comique, the performances during
which Marat and Charlotte Corday were judged. Second,
there is the judicial aspect, which, as we know, was in the
eighteenth century inextricably linked to the theatrical aspect. A trial that was conducted on the stage of the Tuileries
was reenacted at the Opéra-Comique every time the death
of the revolutionary was shown. The two stations also
maintain inverse relations of repetition; the condemnation
of the king is not repeatable but is past recall. The judgment
of Charlotte Corday is re-presentable ad infinitum, or as
many times as the death of Marat is acted on stage. We will
return to this point later.

The judgment of the king, moreover—and this brings us
to the middle stations (2 and 5)—produces a text, the sentence, the effect of which will be the execution of Louis;
without this text, no death would be possible. Marat's
death, or Charlotte Corday's judgment in the theater, is the
effect of a text whose apparent inspiration was the assassination of the People's Friend. Let us consider the place of these
two intermediate stations. The text of Louis XVI's judgment was the trial report and the written resolution that
transformed the word into writing, the logos into law.
Only the writ could authorize the punishment, the *mise à*

mort. The sentence, then, was at once representation and promulgation; it recapitulated and conveyed the judicial deliberations, it anticipated and prescribed the execution. The text conveyed the sentence between the stage and the guillotine. Inversely, the text of the plays about the death of Marat recounted, recapitulated, an execution; in that sense, it can be said that they were a representation. However, the real representation underlying them was the one that would materialize in the theater; hence it is more accurate to regard the theatrical text not as representation but as representability, as a possibility of representation, as a virtual mimesis. Like the text that decided the king's death, the text of Marat's death had a transitional value: it transformed the irremediable (the assassination) into something re-presentable, that is, into a gesture capable of being repeated.

At the other end of the network (3 and 4) are two executions, two violent deaths—the first produced by a text of a judicial nature, the second grounding, in its tragedy, the text to come; one the product of the sentence, the other bearing the sentence within it in a latent form; and yet the one and the other strangely linked together in revolutionary practice, the death of the People's Friend representing a form of expiatory sacrifice for the death of the People's Father.

In the network so defined, various energies circulate, relationships that we must now try to evaluate. The relationship, during the French Revolution, of death to writing and writing to logos—or, inversely, of word to law, and law to execution—not only underlay the revolutionary practice of justice, its obsession with legitimacy, but, conversely, underlay the theatrical practice of the Revolution, whether the latter was manifested in the extraordinary parades of the Fête de la Fédération and the Fête de l'Etre Suprême or in the patriotic demonstrations organized by the leaders. Justice had a purely theatrical side which was explored and illustrated in a striking manner in the public executions, on the one hand, and in the revolutionary tribunals, on the other: a theater of silence, punctuated by the rolling of the drums, as in the scene during which the condemned Louis Capet was not allowed to address his people; and a theater that was extraordinarily verbal, the theater of the trial, where strength of voice, quality of tone, or the mere act of speaking out were so many contributions to the exercise of justice. As for the judicial character of the theater, look at the register of revolutionary plays: *Le Tribunal redoutable* by Martelière, *Le Jugement dernier des rois* by Maréchal, *Le Bienfait de la loi* by Forgeot, *Les Contre-révolutionnaires jugés par eux-mêmes* by Dorvo, *Le Tribunal révolutionnaire* by Ducancel, or that *Ami des lois* that was being talked about the very day of Louis's judgment. The titles may not always have been so explicit, but under the name *Charles X, Les Victimes cloîtrées, Brutus,* or *Robert, chef des brigands* (Schiller's play transformed and adapted to the needs of the Revolution), the formula was still and always a very precise, almost ritual form of trial.

It was no accident that the Commune decided to close all the theaters on the day the king's trial opened;[16] in a sense, it was because the proceedings at the Tuileries theater used up all the theatricality of which the Revolution was capable. Coming within the provisions of a legislation that governed both the regime of the Tribunal and that of the spectacle, the two orders were bound together in the death that engendered them and the reversed production of text and logos that manifested them.

What we have, then, is a network or system comprising a series of functions, presented, for the sake of convenience, in a chronological order which must not be given primary importance; in fact, in this instance the dating does not govern the forces that come into play. Thus the king's execution, or its possibility, was clearly *the cause* of the trial that began on 1 October 1792. "Can a king brought to trial be

16. Jacques Hérissay, *Le Monde des théâtres pendant la Révolution* (Paris: Perrin, 1922), p. 130.

saved?" exclaimed Danton. "He is a dead man when he appears before his judges."[17] What was involved, then—a judicial action, or a ritual based on the anticipated death of Louis? No sooner had the trial gotten underway than Merlin de Thionville declared: "After having decreed the abolition of the royalty, the time has come at last for the Convention to show that a dethroned king is not even a citizen; he must fall under the national sword, and all those who have conspired with him must follow him to the scaffold."[18] Just as the theatrical representation of Marat's death was not framed by any explicit sequence—it was said that one play was written before his assassination—the various events isolated in our network exhibit diachronic links and synchronic relationships.

Taken as a whole, the two series also exhibit a third type of relationship, a mirror-like one: the Marat-Corday trial appears as the reversed image, a faithful and yet alien reflection, of the trial and execution of Louis XVI. One is the "in-another-time-and-place" of the other, the figure of an alienation that transcends the mere action of the law. Doubtless it could be said that the king's trial was the pretext for Marat's assassination, or, again, that the crime cried for vengeance. Garat, whom the Revolution so often confused with Marat, had suggested, on 3 June 1791, that the parricides should have one of their hands cut off; the Girondins, who did not wish for the king's death, were in turn caught in the fatal vise of revolutionary justice. Marat would have to die. But, all things considered, the various systems of representation, or rather, communication, were grounded in the concept of "revolution" in Robespierre's sense, i.e., a complete rotation, the closure of a cycle.

In speaking of the six plays representing Marat's death why is it necessary to evoke a wider system that, although based on parallel structures, goes far beyond the immediate

---

17. See Soboul, *Le Procès de Louis XVI,* p. 24.
18. Soboul, *Le Procès de Louis XVI,* p. 46.

subject? For reasons of methodology, first of all. The aim here is to apply a systemic critique rather than a purely analytical approach, which would be incapable of bringing out the dynamic aspects of spectacle and representation. The elements we are considering pertain not to knowledge but to a structured, loosely ordered communication pieced together from disparate manifestations. It is not that the king's death evokes and obscurely prefigures Marat's; rather, in its judicial and theatrical manifestation, the king's death indefinitely approximates the quasi-royal character of Citizen Marat's death and celebration in the theater. We start from a system, a combinative series of relations *(une combinatoire)* that underlie a variety of functions that operate through the indelible nature of the text and the fragility of the declamation. Are we justified in involving the theater in an ensemble that appears to reach beyond its scope, its significance, its intended purpose? That is what we shall have to consider here.

Commenting on *The Theater and Its Double,* Jacques Derrida reviews some of the main points of Antonin Artaud's impassioned critique of the theatrical practice of the Occident:

The stage is theological for as long as its structure, following the entirety of tradition, comports the following elements: an author-creator, absent and from afar, is armed with a text and keeps watch over, assembles, regulates the time or the meaning of representation, letting this latter *represent* him as concerns what is called the content of his thoughts, his intentions, his ideas. He lets representation represent him through representatives, directors or actors. . . . Who moreover—and this is the ironic rule of the representative structure which organizes all these relationships—creates nothing, has only the illusion of having created, because he only transcribes and makes available for reading a text whose nature is itself necessarily representative; and this representative text maintains with what is called the "real" (the existing real, the "reality" about which Artaud said, in the "Avertissement" to *Le Moine,* that it is an "excrement of the mind") an imitative and reproductive relationship. Finally, the theological stage comports a passive, seated public, a public of spectators, of consumers, of "enjoyers"—as Nietzsche and Artaud both say—attending a production that lacks true volume or depth, a production that is level, offered to their voyeuristic scrutiny.[19]

This indictment of the theological stage assumes an added dimension when it is compared, factually, with the history of the theater under the Revolution. At that time the "distant" authority of the author was strengthened. A series of decrees, dating from 1792, regulated copyrights and so guaranteed the inviolable status of the text; decrees also authorized the author's name to appear on the playbill. Then, the actor unquestionably triumphed in finally obtaining citizenship and voting rights and in attaining a prestige that was almost suspect in the middle of a revolutionary period: an actor's stature would be increased by the text which he had assimilated so well (Talma is an example), and even those less than brilliant were assured of a relatively high degree of visibility. In a sense there was already a certain perversion in this, the actor no longer being the transparency of the text become speech, but, rather, a kind of opacity misappropriating the text and enslaving it to his own theatricality.

This strengthening of the text, the author, and the actor on the stage of '89 was marked by several curious events. During the last years of the Ancien Régime, a series of oppressive measures had been imposed on the little theaters that were thriving under the popular auspices of the Foire Saint-Laurent and the Foire Saint-Germain. Anxious to protect its exclusive status, the Comédie-Française had ob-

19. Jacques Derrida, "The Theater of Cruelty and the Closure of Representation," in *Writing and Difference,* trans. Alan Bass (Chicago: University of Chicago Press, 1978), p. 235.

tained several decrees against rival theater companies. The actors, prohibited from reciting texts, took to singing them; prohibited from singing texts, they began carrying placards displaying their lines; prohibited from using a text in any form, they—naturally—turned to mime. Finally, this series of harassments and responses having proved that the theater could manage quite well without a text—which confirms Artaud's position—and that indigence gives rise to ingenuity, one of the last, and by no means least interesting, forms hit upon was to require that a veil be suspended between the actors and the spectators during the entire performance. Much can be said concerning that veil, which, as we know, did not discourage the public in the least; we will come back to it. What is notable here is the privileged character of the text. The text was bestowed on the theater like a title of nobility on a meritorious family. It is said that on learning of the fall of the Bastille and after official permission had been given to all the theaters to reopen their doors, Plancher-Valcour, director of the Délassements-Comiques, ripped down the notorious veil to the cry: "Vive la Liberté!"

The separation—already symbolized by the veil—between the stage and the spectators was made even greater, a development Voltaire welcomed and Diderot deplored. The stage cleared of spectators, their passive role carefully monitored, the primacy of the text reestablished along with the dignity of the author, the actor's respectability assured—everything, in that incredible mushrooming of theaters that occurred between 1789 and 1793, seems to indicate that in the midst of the liberating chaos of the Revolution the most oppressive elements of the "theological stage" were set in place.

The oppressive primacy of the text and the increased distance between stage and spectators were manifestations of the new revolutionary theater, a model or forerunner of that rigid theater that Artaud believed had been emptied of its meaning and vitality by the Occident. They were also signs of the theaters' liberation between 1789 and 1793—and this is only a seeming paradox, for the privileged status of the text, like the right of property, was a revolutionary conquest, and along with that privilege a quasi-sacred enclosure, suitable for the rite that was to unfold within it, was set up between the stage and an increasingly constrained public. One can see, then, that it is impossible to consider the revolutionary theater without examining, once more, the status of the theatrical text. Where is the text to be placed in an extra-literary genre that plays simultaneously upon speech, interpretation, space, and repetition?[20] How does one go about studying the theater, seeing that it is at once a ritual of gestures, an enclosed repetition, a reading aloud, a book torn between the *mise en scène* and the *mise en page,* the former taking the place of the latter? In its organization, the theater embodies a revolution. Confronted with this revolution, there are several critical strategies to choose from: for example, a semiology of a theater whose text would be practically disregarded—a study of entrances and exits, spaces, stage settings, movements, and lighting. The text would then be an accessory comparable to the curtain that is raised at the beginning of each act and lowered at the end of the performance. It unveils and conceals, like one of the stock costumes of an itinerant theatrical company. One can also privilege the text at the expense of its intended use in the theater, reading it as a self-contained object and thereby mutilating it. After all, since there is a written text, every reading of it is legitimate; it will also be said in this case that a particular theater is better adapted to reading than to the stage, and so on. Analysis is possible in both cases, but it seems to obliterate the specific ambiguity of the theatrical text.

20. Anne Ubersfeld has offered a reading of the theatrical text that tries to reconcile the intended scenic destination of the writing and its linguistic formulation. See *Lire le théâtre* (Paris: Editions Sociales, 1978). The reverse problem, the theatricality of the narrative text, is explored in an exemplary way by Peter Brooks, *The Melodramatic Imagination* (New Haven, Conn.: Yale University Press, 1976).

What is the theatrical text? How does the *mise en scène* for which it is intended influence the *mise en page* where it is set and read before being declaimed? Are the relationships of theatrical writing and representation entirely encompassed within the general relationships of writing and mimesis? Is this transience from written text to logos unique, and does this aspect alone suffice to set the theatrical text apart as a writing whose function differs radically from all other textual operations? These are questions which, while admitting of no easy answers, should be kept in mind. The reflections below will begin to address them.

In his commentary on Artaud, Derrida speaks of the theatrical text as one "whose nature is itself necessarily representative, [a text which] maintains with what is called the 'real' an imitative and reproductive relationship."[21] Yet, what ultimately imitates and reproduces is quite as much the stage, the décor, the movement, the costumes, and so forth. Could it not be said that the fundamental difference between the theatrical text and other writing lies not in the representation it defines but in the possibility to which it lends itself of being the object of a representation? The theatrical text is not representation inscribed in language but future representation on the stage. It is the representability of the theatrical text that makes it, in a certain sense, unreadable and allows it endlessly to be recited aloud, rehearsed, presented, and represented. In this sense theatrical writing, even in the tradition of the West, is not the essence of a certain mode of representation, as Artaud lamented, but, rather, what postpones that representation, at the same time making it possible and deferring it. Between the event that is called the assassination of Jean-Paul Marat and the event called the representation, in the theater, of the death of Jean-Paul Marat, writing is at once remembrance and anticipation; more than a fragile link, it is a delay, it is lapse, possibility,

21. Derrida, "The Theater of Cruelty," in *Writing and Difference,* p. 235.

the putting off, till the morrow, of Marat's inevitable execution by Charlotte Corday.

Rooted in the classical *episteme,* the language of the Revolution is, to be sure, still the language of Order, of autocracy, of indubitable representation. In that *episteme,* theatrical writing develops the possibility of representation with a kind of tragic serenity. The aleatory character that accompanies the concept of possibility should not be taken lightly. Between the exercise of theatrical writing and the eventuality of the staging is a wait that is charged with meaning and no less dramatic (that is, theatrical) than the twenty-four hours that were to separate the written sentence of the king's death and his public execution. Hence this aspect of the theatrical text—its alienation, its having-to-be-spoken—does not have its reference in actual experience but in an experience yet to come; a text set down on a page to which it will perhaps be given to become life, speech, presence, but only within the strictly delimited enclosure of theatrical illusion. Marat's actual death counts for little in these lines written in anticipation of the performance to come. That a certain play was written before the assassination scarcely modifies the idea of a diachronic plausibility. That representations of this assassination took great "liberties" with factual reality merely—paradoxically—confirms the genre's alienation, for the theater does not function in terms of actual experience but always with an eye to a to-be-experienced. Marat's death in the theater is, eternally, his rebirth.

The question of the representability of the text naturally inspires a chain of inquiries. On what premises does the possibility of representation depend? For example: just after the Assembly had voted for the king's death, a monarchist took his revenge on Lepelletier de Saint-Fargeau. Paris was moved by the event and David did a touching portrayal of the assassinated deputy. A few months later, Charlotte Corday stabbed Jean-Paul Marat; David depicted the scene in a painting that became famous and a series of plays was pre-

sented in the theater in honor of this new martyr. During the
Revolution, David did another highly successful painting,
The Death of Titus, inspired by classical antiquity but intended for an entirely contemporary sensibility. Some actors, taking advantage of its popularity, made it into a *tableau vivant.* [22] It will be necessary to examine the relationships that obtained in the revolutionary aesthetic, the vision
or speech that was implanted by increasingly violent deaths.

To account for the text in its "theatricality," that is, its
representability, is not to account for the theatrical phenomenon, however. Just as it appeared inadequate to treat the
theatrical text as the privileged instrument of representation, it seems inadequate to consider the theater as an auton-
omous mechanism governed by the stage, the actor, the
curtain, or the audience. By virtue of its properly social
character—popular assembly, pageant, game, ritual—the
theater fully pertains to what can be called a sociology of
history, in what I have designated a network of communica-
tions. One would need to envisage a study of the revolutionary theater comparable to the one Mona Ozouf did on
the revolutionary *fête;* [23] that is, a study of the revolutionary
theater that would not be simply a recounting of its avatars
but the observation of its functions, its space, its time, its
integral participation in revolutionary life. Such a study
would go beyond the present one. Our observation will be
confined to the perspectives from which a given theatrical
event is grounded in a particular history, to the relationships
the plays I have selected maintain with the development of
the regime, and to the nature of the theatrical functions that
appear simultaneously in the tribunal and on the stage, on
the side of law or comic illusion. That is why, in the case I
propose to study here, we will focus our inquiry on the
judicial function.

22. Hérissay, *Le Monde des théâtres,* p. 86.
23. Mona Ozouf, *La Fête révolutionnaire* (Paris: Gallimard, 1976).

This focus will not limit the sociological impact of the theater or its historicity. On the contrary, I will try to demonstrate how the same dynamic comes into play between the formulation of the law and the promulgation of the text, and how the same symbolic order applies to participants and spectators alike. There is no need to retrace the history of punishment before and during the Revolution. Michel Foucault, in *Discipline and Punish,* has amply shown how there functioned, on the stage of "the theater of terror,"[24] a judicial system intelligible to the senses. This "punitive theater" still functioned during the Revolution and the stamp of royal justice continued to be visible. But the execution of Louis XVI, owing to the void it created at the summit of the judicial organization, brought about a disequilibrium that was to affect both the theater of punishment and punishment in the theater. We shall thus have to consider the ties that were formed or drawn closer in the context of justice, in the promulgation of the law, the word, or the sentence; ties that no longer linked with the Grève—and this was one of the signs of the new times—but with the tribunal.

To return to our network of communication: between January and July 1793, between the king's execution and the assassination of Jean-Paul Marat, the Revolutionary Tribunal was formally established. In the course of the meeting of 12 March, Marat exclaimed: "One has done nothing so long as one has not torn away the veil. You have wisely ordered a revolutionary tribunal to be set up; it will be the bulwark of Liberty."[25] Ironically, less than a month later Marat was called before this same tribunal, but was acquitted. The Revolutionary Tribunal made it possible to establish in the closed space of judgment, in the arena of punishment, what both enabled the theater to function and betrayed dramatic

24. Michel Foucault, *Discipline and Punish,* trans. Alan Sheridan (New York: Pantheon Books, 1977), p.49.

25. Session of 15 March 1793, *Le Moniteur,* no.74.

illusion. That the judicial system called on all the formal elements of the theater should not be seen as a fanciful stroke on the part of the legislators; that the theater in turn became the tumultuous tribunal of the Revolution was indeed a manifestation of its rootedness in historicity.

Let us complete our network:

1. The trial of Louis XVI   6. The theatrical repre-
                                sentation of Marat's
2. The sentence   death
3. The king's execution   5. The theatrical text
                             4. Marat's assassination

[Setting up of the Revolutionary Tribunal; Marat tried and acquitted]

The king was judged a few weeks before the setting up of the Revolutionary Tribunal; Marat was acquitted by that same tribunal a few weeks before his assassination by Charlotte Corday. In our network the setting up of the tribunal plays the role of an interchange of the sort posited by Michel Serres:

> It is a multiple nexus without an intersection, or, if you will, an intersection without a junction or crossroads. It receives and distributes, it sorts out without mixing, it simulates, locally, at a pinpoint station, the entirety of the efferent and afferent network. In this sense it is in effect the local projection of the total network.[26]

Our schema is now almost complete. Between the fixed point of the killing, the *mise à mort,* and the moving point of the representation, revolutionary symbolism operates in its fulfillment and its virtuality. The routes communicate via the interchange, the impassible nexus of the Revolutionary

26. Michel Serres, *L'Interférence* (Paris: Editions de Minuit, 1972), p. 131.

Tribunal. It only remains to unravel patiently the tangle of functions that draw together the moving poles of revolutionary activity, of which the theater is more a terminal connection than a culmination. This network carries a multiplicity of intentions, utterances, and messages.[27] The public character of the new constitution is reaffirmed at every stage. The proclamation of the law, the posting of the sentence, the admission of the public to the most serious deliberations of the Assembly—in all its activities the Revolution demands a reader, a listener, ultimately, a spectator. This spectator tirelessly covers the whole network, and so we must find out who he is.

27. I have limited myself here to plays that were performed fairly frequently and were important enough to have been reviewed in the various revolutionary newspapers. Hérissay mentions the following titles: *La Mort de Marat, La Mort de l'infortuné Marat, Marat dans le souterrain des Cordeliers, L'Apothéose de Marat et Lepelletier, Marat dans l'Olympe, L'Arrivée de Marat aux Champs-Elysées, Le Véritable Ami du Peuple* (*Le Monde des théâtres,* pp. 144–45).

2

The Spectator

The network I have described as pertinent for studying the theatrical function is one based on communication. Before examining the structure of the network and the avatars of the circuit—the excesses, the deficiencies—we must try to discover what happens with regard to the receiver, that familiar other person who listens, reads, strolls in the Place de Grève or gets jostled in the galleries of the Assembly, that essential anonymous figure without whom the network would be meaningless: the spectator. For reasons that will, I hope, be justified later on, we will not distinguish between the public that watches an execution and the one that attends a theatrical performance. It is not the nature of the perception that interests us here—the horror experienced in witnessing the execution, the pleasure felt in seeing the play— but only the function of the spectator.

"In the ceremonies of the public execution," writes Michel Foucault, "the main character was the people, whose real and immediate presence was required for the performance. An execution that was known to be taking place, but which did so in secret, would scarcely have had any meaning."[1] Everyone is familiar with the arguments in favor of capital punishment because it is exemplary, and consequently, for a visible punishment so that the lesson to be learned will be engraved in the memory of the spectator. During the long debates of the summer of 1791 on the death

1. Michel Foucault, *Discipline and Punish,* trans. Alan Sheridan (New York: Pantheon Books, 1977), pp. 57–58.

penalty, the spectacle of the scaffold, and the official nature
of punishment, the position held by the deputies was identical to the one that had been applied for centuries by the royal
courts. Lepelletier de Saint-Fargeau vigorously restated it in
the meeting of 3 June: "The principle of all punishment is
that it must repress by example; therefore it must not be
secret."[2] Dutau, anxious to preserve the exemplary force of
the death penalty and, like his colleagues, wanting to abolish torture, proposed a veritable *mise en scène,* a show whose
complex ceremony would make up for the diminished cruelty of the execution:

> If you want the death penalty—reduced simply to the depriva-
> tion of life, reserved for the murderer whom no motive excuses,
> and above all, free of torture—to retain all its exemplary effective-
> ness, to act as a useful influence on morals, and to become a salu-
> tary lesson to those who are drawn irresistibly to crime by a secret
> penchant, make the punishment of the guilty into an imposing
> spectacle; link the execution to a doleful and most touching dis-
> play; let that terrible day be a national day of mourning; let the
> general suffering be depicted strikingly. Imagine the forms that are
> most compatible with a tender sensibility; interest the hearts of all
> in the fate of the luckless one who will come under the sword of
> justice, so that he will be offered solace on every side; and let his
> miserable remains receive the honors of burial. Let the magistrate
> robed in black crepe announce to the people the crime and the sad
> necessity of a legal retribution. Let the different scenes of this
> *tragedy* make an impression on all the senses, stirring every gentle
> and honest affection; let them inspire the most saint-like respect for
> the life of men; let them wring tears of repentance from the wicked;
> lastly, let them call forth the most moral reflections and all the civic
> feelings.[3]

As we see, far from being frightened by the disturbances
that had accompanied a number of public executions (dis-

2. Session of the Assembly, 3 June 1791, *Le Moniteur,* no. 154.
3. Ibid. (my italics).

turbances which in a practical sense contributed, perhaps, to the separation of the condemned man from his public), the legislators increased the presence and necessity of the people in their judicial reform. Many studies have cited examples of executions in which the crowd took an active part, either by reinforcing royal justice through attacks on a condemned man ill-protected by his guards, or, on the contrary, by trying in every way to save him from the scaffold. The political interpretation to be put upon these spontaneous actions is not as self-evident as it first appears: to imagine a capricious public sympathizing with the accused or overwhelming him with its fury as a result of a politicization that remains to be established does not suffice to explain the real function of the spectator at the end of the eighteenth century. Michel Foucault mentions an execution that took place shortly after the corn riot, in the course of which the soldiers formed a barrier between the prisoners about to be executed and the public: "No one was allowed onto the Grève during the execution. . . . Whatever the part played by feelings of humanity for the condemned in the abandonment of the liturgy of public executions, there was, in any case, on the part of state power, a political fear of the effects of these ambiguous rituals."[4] Whatever the preoccupation of monarchical justice may have been during the last years of Louis XVI's reign, in 1791 the legislators had one idea in mind: to strengthen, or restore, the link between death presented as a spectacle and the public for whom that death was ultimately justified. Thus the assembly decided to adopt decapitation in preference to hanging because, according to an unnamed deputy:

Punishments ought to be considered (1) not with regard to the guilty, but (2) with regard to the interests of society; now, the interests of society lie in setting a great example. The spectator must return home filled with terror. I do not believe that behead-

4. Foucault, *Discipline and Punish,* p. 65.

ing as a form of execution is physically harsher than the gallows; but it has the advantage, for society, of being more frightening.[5]

One could hardly express more clearly and forcefully that revolutionary justice was inscribed in a system of communication, rather than a system of values, and that the spectacle death offered the spectator was a message the exchange of which constituted the law. With this in mind, it is interesting to note that the main actor, the guilty party, was sacrificed, in every sense, for the benefit of the audience, the public. That the legislators of '91 seemed more concerned with the readability of the message than with its content was also in the order of revolutionary justice.

It is certain, then, that under the Revolution punishment was still organized, or conceived of, as a spectacle. Michel Foucault has done an exhaustive analysis of the symbolism that surrounded the ritual of execution and the possibility, offered by the ritual, of reaffirming both the order on which the execution was based and the exemplary nature of the *mise à mort.* What was described, and what was expressed on the benches of the Assembly in June 1791, was an intentionality or, to put it another way, the need for a public, a receiver. But once this need is established, can the spectator be defined in terms of the message addressed to him? Is one entitled to imagine a different public according to whether the condemned was an aristocrat or an artisan, or according to whether the execution took place on the Grève or on the stage of a traveling theater? In other words, perhaps the content of the message—the purpose of the spectacle, the exemplarity of the execution—ought not to be permitted to define the place of the spectator. This fusion is at the origin of most studies on the nature of theatrical pleasure, the nature of the (more complex) pleasure of the aficionado, and so on. However fascinating these studies may be, they remain incomplete.

5. Session of the Assembly, 4 June 1791, *Le Moniteur,* no. 155.

Just because every actor requires, for the time of a performance, that he be conceded a make-believe reality, and
because the whole display with which he surrounds himself
tends to uphold that reality, are we to imagine that a spectator leaves his reason and common sense at the theater entrance, in an exercise of "suspension of disbelief" miraculously synchronized with the actor's performance? If so, one
would need to analyze the pleasure of the spectator of comedy, or melodrama, farce, tragedy, poetry recital, torture,
hangings, mass parades, festivals, and so on. One would
need to bring out the distinctions among the various sensa-
tions experienced, and to trace the workings of the imagination. Even when the entire range of these diverse subjectivi-
ties has been covered, however, one would still not have
determined in what, precisely, the function of the spectator
consists. Therefore, instead of defining the spectator in relation to the intent of the spectacle designed for him, I will
focus directly on the audience in its receptive availability
and try to see how its function is organized in terms, not of
the message's content, but of its transmissibility alone.

It seems in fact that this first separation between the condemned man and the public (Michel Foucault cites an example dating from 1775) was contemporaneous with a comparable separation between the actor and the spectator in the
theater. The part Voltaire played in the exclusion of the
public from the stage is well known; this exclusion was
preceded and followed by a considerable distancing that
included, among other measures, the intrusion of armed
guards. According to Diderot, the theatrical atmosphere
underwent a transformation in the course of the eighteenth
century:

Fifteen years ago our theaters were tumultuous places. The cool-
est heads got overheated on entering and reasonable men more or
less shared the transports of the mad. . . . People became agitated,
moved about, pushed one another, spirits went wild. What mood
could be more favorable to a poet? The play commenced with
difficulty and was interrupted often, but when a good part was

reached. . . . The enthusiasm went from the floor to the tiers, and from the tiers to the boxes. The people had arrived flushed with excitement; they left the theater intoxicated. . . . It was like a storm that would dissipate far in the distance, a storm whose rumbling would last long after it had moved on. That was pleasure. Nowadays people arrive cold, they listen cold, and I don't know where they go. Those insolent fusiliers stationed to the right and to the left in order to temper the transports of my admiration, my sensibility, and my joy, making our theaters into places quieter and more proper than our churches, offend me extraordinarily.[6]

These comments express a first paradox to which we will return: namely, the longing for a spectacle in which all theatrical illusion is dispensed with, in which no suspension of disbelief is required, and in which the spectator adds to the play; moreover, they describe a theatrical pleasure freed from the imposition of a make-believe reality.

A passage from *Jacques le fataliste,* in which Diderot outlines what must be one of the most penetrating commentaries on the function of the spectator, explicates this idea:

What, to your way of thinking, is the motive that attracts people to public executions? Inhumanity? You are wrong: the masses are not inhuman. That unfortunate wretch about whose gallows they gather—they would snatch him from the hands of justice if they could. They go to the Grève rather to find a scene that they can retell upon their return to their district. This scene or the other, it matters not, so long as the people can play a role, gather their neighbors about them, and make themselves heard. Give them an amusing gala on the boulevards, and you will see that the execution square will be empty. The people are mad for spectacle, and they rush to spectacles because they are amused by watching them, and still more amused by the retelling they do upon their return.[7]

6. Denis Diderot, "Réponse à la lettre de Madame Riccoboni," in *Oeuvres* (Paris: Gallimard, Bibliothèque de la Pléiade, 1951), p. 1288.

7. Denis Diderot, *Jacques the Fatalist and His Master,* trans. J. Robert Long (New York: W. W. Norton, 1978), p. 166.

These lines, as far as I know the only ones to be equally concerned with the spectator of the judicial action and that of the aesthetic work, establish two important points. (1) The acclaimed exemplarity of the death penalty is a wasted lesson. What interests the spectator is the spectacle per se. His position as a receiver is established, constituted, made use of, independently of the significance of the message received. There is not one public thirsting for blood and tortures and another public eager for entertainments and pleasures; a public is formed the moment there is a spectacle. A public execution and a puppet show will interest the same spectator.

(2) The second point is no less important: Diderot suggests that the spectator-receiver's raison d'être lies in the possibility of a transmutation from the role of receiver to that of actor. To retell is to act. Whether a first-order representation (the "reality" of the public execution) or a second-order representation (the theatrical staging of an execution) is involved is of no real importance to the spectator, who uses the occasion to collect the material of a representation to come, that of retelling, playing a role, assembling the neighbors and getting them to listen. Diderot is here describing the formation of a *mise en scène,* a "rehearsal" properly speaking, in which the spectator ultimately finds his justification: to have become an actor. Perhaps it is from this point of view that many of the public incidents cited by Michel Foucault, in the course of which the people took an active part in the unfolding of justice, must be "read": "As the executioner was carrying out the execution, the local fish-wives walked in procession, holding aloft an effigy of the condemned man, and then cut off [its] head." Foucault adds, "The people had to bring its assistance to the King."[8] This assistance, as I interpret it, was not necessarily of an ideological nature but was based on the latent and desired

8. Foucault, *Discipline and Punish,* p. 59.

reversibility of the position of spectator. This reversibility inherent in the receiver function may also explain the fact that the people occasionally snatched victims from the executioners; this was perhaps not a matter of a political orientation that led the public to manifest indulgence, compassion, or a spirit of revenge, but, rather, another possibility of participating in the spectacle offered it.

Clearly, this perspective is opposed to the kind of retrospective ideological analysis that would make the people of Paris into a politicized, albeit unpredictable, body, sometimes siding with the law and sometimes going against it, in a childish, touching, brutal, or irrational manner. This is not to say that the lower classes were not politicized but, rather, that being put in the position of spectator signifies being put in a necessarily political position. Diderot's spectator is an actor "in waiting," an incomplete figure who is preparing for a role he too will play and whose model he looks at with eagerness. Hence "to attend" means "to prepare for." Inherent in the notion of the spectator is that of the future actor; part of the pleasure of the spectacle lies in anticipation of another spectacle in which the spectator will finally be actor. To appeal to an audience is to appeal to this possibility of a spectator-actor exchange, and an audience that does not achieve this exchange, this cycle, this transformation, is a mutilated audience—or, one might say, an alienated one.

We know that Diderot, influenced by the theories of Abbé Du Bos, privileged seeing in the theater. In order to immerse oneself more thoroughly in the spectacle, he suggested that one should not only concentrate on the vision offered but also stop one's ears (mutilation of the senses) so that no sound would distract one's attention from the main element, the spectacle. Rousseau on the other hand, suggested covering one's eyes so that nothing would interrupt the pleasure of hearing the spoken lines. We are not concerned here with deciding who best grasped the meaning of the theater; in either case the spectator is determined not only as a passive being but, further, and at times voluntarily, as an incomplete being. The suspension of disbelief represents another, more serious form of mutilation, that of reason or common sense. At times blind, at times deaf, of necessity mute, sacrificing his autonomy or his integrity in the hope of a specific and deferred pleasure: this is the profile of the spectator, a personage endlessly waiting to be. In other words, reception of a message cannot occur without requiring a form of alienation, itself being extraneous to the form or the content of the message that is transmitted.

One better understands, then, that the Revolution's constant concern with making the people into a public did not necessarily correspond to any form of political liberalism; that this objective was political in nature is beyond doubt, but it was inscribed in a tradition that consists in repressing by means of the spectacle. To make a spectator of the people, while making sure that the possibility of a spectator-actor reversibility remains carefully controlled, is to maintain an alienation that is the real form of power. The Freedom of Theaters legislation (13 January 1791) that made it possible to count nearly forty-five theaters and three puppet theaters a few months later was also a means of constituting a larger public that was to be an object of continual surveillance. The Assembly's constant preoccupation with everything touching upon the theatrical phenomenon was an entirely political preoccupation. Freedom of theaters, followed by freedom of festivals, did not eliminate complex regulations: certain plays were ordered performed free of charge for the edification of the public, and a carefully staged participation of a few spectators was even arranged in advance. Thus, during the performance of *Les Victimes cloîtrées* [*The Cloistered Victims*] by Monvel, on 29 March 1791, a spectator rose up and demanded the immediate arrest of the character Père Laurent, saying that he knew the man personally. This kind of disturbance was organized in every detail, and fooled people only once. It came to be forbidden to carry arms at the theater and, at the same time, the number of *fêtes* was increased, these being a unique variation of the spectacle in which the public was authorized to combine—within the established rules of conduct—the roles of actor and spectator. It is interesting to note that on the one hand "the closed chamber soon became the emblem of counter-revolutionary designs" so that national festivals "could have no other enclosure than the canopy of the sky,"[9] and that, on the other hand, the course of the processions, the order of the parades, the sequence of the chariots and the performances were all rigorously determined. The revolutionary *fête* seems, therefore, to have merged the strictly political requirement of a passive spectator with the requirement inherent in every spectator that he be a participant, hence an actor, as well. Instituting the Festival of the Supreme Being was not the least of Robespierre's political acts.

Theoretical texts on the theater were abundant in the eighteenth century. Still one of the most interesting is the work by Sébastien Mercier, if only for this brief remark placing the spectator firmly in a group or class context: "Every spectator," he says, "judges as a public man and not simply as a private individual; he puts aside both his interests and his prejudices; he is just toward himself, and it is a fact that in the long run the people are the fairest judges."[10] Apart from the now-familiar association of the figure of the spectator with that of the judge, this remark fits squarely in the ideological tradition of the *Social Contract,* with Rousseau's definition of the relationship between the citizen and the sovereign, the particular will and the general will. In Book Two of the *Social Contract* Rousseau distinguishes particular interests—which are individual, egotistical, likely to be prejudicial to the interests of others—from the general will—which, once particular interests are canceled

9. Mona Ozouf, *La Fête révolutionnaire* (Paris: Gallimard, 1976), pp. 151, 152. On the *fête* and the revolutionary theater, see also Frederick Brown, *Theater and Revolution* (New York: Viking Press, 1980).

10. Sébastien Mercier, *Du théâtre* (Amsterdam: E. Van Harrevelt, 1773), p. 203.

because they are in perpetual contradiction—necessarily represents the desire for the general welfare. "It is the overlap among different interests that creates the social bond," writes Rousseau, concluding: "The general will is always well-intentioned, it always looks to the public good."[11]

It is not a question here of evaluating the correctness of Rousseau's political reasoning but of examining the possibility, suggested by Mercier, of a theoretical public, a group or class whose judgment would necessarily be right. Clearly, this public was those very people whom the legislators of '91 invited to the deliberations of the juries as a guarantor of justice and a protection of the innocent; however, they were carefully separated from the spectacle to which they were exposed, they were subjected to a rule of silence, and they were constantly held to the passive role of spectators. A political force, an alienated force, the revolutionary public was perhaps not that simple-minded, hungry, sanguinary, and generous crowd that was described in the eighteenth century, but a complex and indispensable dimension of the communication network that functioned and expanded between 1789 and 1795. Of the actionalist analysis in history, Alain Touraine writes:

> The social significance of an action must not be confused with the meaning the actor gives it. When one insists on establishing this significance at the most superficial level, one is forced to resort to mechanical explanations whenever diversity of opinions and behaviors appears. On the contrary, it is necessary to reach a social collective consciousness, which does not coincide with individual consciousnesses, and so presents itself as an unconscious.[12]

It may be useful at this point to move away from examples from the revolutionary period in order to look more

11. Jean-Jacques Rousseau, *The Social Contract,* trans. Wilmoore Kendall (Chicago: Henry Regnery Company, 1954), pp. 33, 38.
12. Alain Touraine, *Sociologie de l'action* (Paris: Editions du Seuil, 1965), p. 26.

closely at the psychical elements that are brought into play in the spectator function.

What Lévi-Strauss says concerning magic could also be said of the spectacle in general:

> There is no reason to doubt the efficacy of magical practices. But at the same time we see that the efficacy of magic implies a belief in magic. The latter has three complementary aspects: first, the sorcerer's belief in the effectiveness of his techniques; second, the patient's or victim's belief in the sorcerer's power; and finally, the faith and expectations of the group, which constantly act as a sort of gravitational field within which the relationship between sorcerer and bewitched is located and defined. [13]

This statement of the problem ties together two elements that I consider inseparable: belief and power. The three aspects of belief submitted by Lévi-Strauss are, indeed, comparable to some of the facts we have noted: the legislators' belief in the exemplarity of the death penalty and the revolutionary value of theater; the actor's belief in his own interpretation, that is, his conviction that he can actually *be* an actor, and the public's complicity, which, although more diffuse, nonetheless involves acceptance of the validity of these two beliefs, an acceptance that is also the recognition of a power, a manipulation, at times an oppression. This acceptance poses a problem. Can one submit in good faith to the mutilated role of spectator, merely in the hope of the spectator-actor reversal suggested by Diderot? The public's belief in, or submission to, the spectacle offered it by what was essentially a political authority during the Revolution bears comparison with the kind of belief to which Octave Mannoni devoted an essay entitled "I Know . . . But All the Same."[14] Exploring the notion of *Verleugnung* (disavowal,

13. Claude Lévi-Strauss, "Magic and Religion," in *Structural Anthropology,* trans. Claire Jacobson and Brooke Grundfest Schoepf (New York: Basic Books, 1963), p.168.

14. Octave Mannoni, "Je sais bien . . . mais quand même," in *Clefs pour l'imaginaire* (Paris: Editions du Seuil, 1969), pp. 14–18.

repudiation), Mannoni writes: "The subject of this study is belief: for example, the belief that allowed the Jews to believe in the existence of Baal without having any faith in him"[15]—in other words, a belief that overrides every form of demystification. Mannoni furnishes a particularly striking example for our purposes, drawn from Talayesva's book, *Sun Chief*:

> The masks of the Hopi are called Katcinas. At a certain time of the year they make an appearance in the pueblos the way Père Noël appears at Christmastime. . . . At the time of initiation, in the course of ceremonies which could not be any more impressive and which directly evoke castration, the adults, those who in the Hopi kinship system are called fathers and uncles, take off their masks, revealing that it was they who played the Katcinas. . . . What is truly bewildering, is that this ceremony, and the disappointing revelation inflicted on the belief in Katcinas, will be the institutional foundation of the new belief in Katcinas, which constitutes the essential part of Hopi religion. The reality—the Katcinas are the fathers and uncles—has to be repudiated through a transformation of the belief. . . . The Hopi can say in good faith, and in a way that is not exactly that which one encounters in psychoanalysis: "I know that the Katcinas are not spirits, they are my fathers and uncles, but all the same the Katcinas are there when my fathers and uncles dance with masks on.[16]

Mannoni's comment is that "belief in the presence of the phallus in the mother is the first belief to be repudiated and the model of all other repudiations."[17]

What most interests him, however, is the role of the uninitiated and mystified children. "An essential ingredient of every initiation is that one solemnly pledges to keep the secret. The initiates will in turn participate in the mystification, and one can say that the children are the support, as it were, of the adults' belief."[18] And he adds: "This derives from an idea that first struck me as a manifest fact in another investigation in which I was trying to discover what

15. Ibid., p. 14.   16. Ibid., p. 16.   17. Ibid., p. 17.   18. Ibid., p. 18.

might sustain the spectators' belief in the theater."[19] It could be said that what is really at issue here, more than a question of belief, is a question of power, a power, however, inextricably linked to belief and perhaps even a condition of that belief. In the initiation procedure of the Hopi, which strongly recalls castration, it is the discovery of the father and the law that takes hold; the belief in the Katcinas "all the same" is accompanied by a submission to a power of which the father is henceforth the disguised image, a power even greater than that of the father. The father or uncle served as the practical support of the power of the Katcinas by lending them a sort of materiality; as a result, the father and the uncle have greater authority for being recognized as the Katcinas' intermediaries. There is no need to recall the infantilization of the people by monarchichal authority: for centuries the king was the Father of the People at the same time that he was the incarnation of divine or civil law. This law was imposed on a public whose submission doubtless stemmed from a collective unconscious comparable to the one Mannoni analyzes, and whose situation always reveals the exercise of an active power.

In other terms, the Hopi example suggests that every transformation or maintenance of belief despite the contradiction of reality operates by way of a situation, a ritual, in which power is at work. It may well be that this power depicts the castration rite, the discovery of the law, that it takes root in the unconscious of a people; the fact is that the initiate, the child, the public, the spectator takes his place and derives his significance from being put in a situation that remains a regulated confrontation with order. Peter Brook describes the stage as "the arena where a living confrontation can take place."[20] Here, as in Diderot's commentary, the reversibility of spectator into actor is latent. The child subjected to initiation buys the promise of in turn being an

19. Ibid.
20. Peter Brook, *The Empty Space* (New York: Atheneum, 1978), p. 99.

initiator; the secrecy surrounding the rites is the guarantee that the power that is at work will be transmitted.

Thus, little by little, the basic elements of the makeup and function of the spectator emerge. In the first place, belief in the message makes possible the link between the spectacle and the public, and, above all, this belief—which may have its model in the unconscious—always involves the acceptance of a power, that of the father, order, the word, or the law. Moreover, this belief and acceptance are tied to the possibility of a reversal of roles, to the initiated child's latent hope of being in turn the possessor of a secret, hence of being in the position of initiator.

The reversibility implied in the spectator situation was not overlooked by revolutionary authority; it was doubtless one of its most serious preoccupations. But here the theater, even more than the execution square, maintains in its structure the security of the status quo. What is demanded of the spectator is the silence that shows his attention; what is expected of him is his approval, in the form of applause, at the end of the play. There were tumultuous performances, to be sure—of *L'Ami des lois* and *L'Ami du Peuple,* for example—but, spectacular as they were, they remained an exception. "One is surprised," writes Jacques Hérissay, "as we arrive at this date of 1791, by the great calm that has abruptly taken the place of the storms that marked the beginning of the Revolution; the spectators seem to have resumed their habits of former times and are content to applaud the principles in vogue, without resorting to the tumultuous outbursts that accompanied *Charles IX* and *Brutus.*"[21] During the session of 13 January 1791, Le Chapelier called attention to the altered situation:

No doubt you have often been scandalized by those armed satellites who are inside the auditoriums and who place the signs of

---

21. Jacques Hérissay, *Le Monde des théâtres pendant la Révolution* (Paris: Perrin, 1922), pp. 99–100.

slavery and constraint beside the citizens' peaceable pleasure. It is surely necessary that order and tranquillity reign in places where many people assemble; it may occasionally be necessary to employ public force to calm people who seek to cause trouble, and to see that regulations are observed; but that does not necessitate that bayonets surround the spectator and that all eyes encounter signs of distrust and armed authority.[22]

The Assembly or the Commune always reacted at once to any disruption in a theater. In 1790, that is, when the Revolution was still engaged in its great movement of liberation, this notice was posted on theater doors: "In pursuance of the orders of the municipality, the public is advised that no person shall enter with canes, staffs, swords, or any kind of offensive arms."[23] This measure was duly commented on by the journalist Prudhomme: "This prohibition was approved of by former police inspectors and other old fogeys of that ilk. . . . " Prudhomme goes on to cite La Fontaine's fable of the simpleton who was a bad judge of the police. In this fable, the lion (the People) wants to marry a maiden (Liberty). The maiden's father (the magistrates) says to him: "Monsieur, you have my permission, but your teeth and your claws (the rights of man and his canes) might harm the young lady; let those trifles be removed or trimmed and your pleasure will be the greater." The lion agrees to this. When those trifles are trimmed, the knaves (the Praetorian Guard) and yard dogs (the police spies) are unleashed on him, leaving him in no condition to wed the maiden.[24]

Thus the continual surveillance of the revolutionary public was interpreted at the time as an excessive use of authority. The Assembly closed the theaters at the slightest disturbance; similarly, public access to all stages of the judicial process was legislated with particular care, and the requisite

22. Cited in ibid., p. 101.
23. Ibid., p. 84.
24. Ibid., pp. 84–85.

passivity, the unconditional submission, of the spectator was strictly defined. Two articles enacted in March 1791 issued the following decrees:

Article I. Citizens who attend hearings of the justices of peace, those of the district tribunals and the criminal tribunals, and those of the police and of commerce, shall sit bareheaded and shall remain respectful and silent. Everything ordered by the judges for the maintenance of order will be enforced without delay.

Article II. If one or more spectators break the silence, give signs of approval or disapproval, either with regard to the defense or with regard to the prosecution, or cause or excite disturbance in any manner whatsoever, and if, after being warned by the bailiffs, they do not immediately return to order, they will be enjoined to leave; and should it be the case that someone shows the least resistance to that injunction, the rebellious individual will be seized at once and removed to the house of detention, where he will remain for twenty-four hours. [25]

Note that in its concern to prevent the reversibility of the spectator-actor role—in this instance, the public-judge or public-jury role—the Assembly offered another public-actor reversibility, that is, from public to accused, thereby closing the system. When the Assembly decided on 10 March 1794, to reopen the Theater of the Nation, under the name Theater of the People, the strictest regulation concerned not the actors or the content of the plays presented but the public. The Assembly decreed that only those citizens carrying identification cards issued by the municipality to "true patriots" would have the right to enter. This decree, in its simplicity and its severity, symbolized the degree to which the public was considered a danger with which to be reckoned. Thus preoccupation with equality—which required the very architecture of the auditorium to be modified so that the placement of all the spectators' seats

25. Session of 1 March 1791, *Le Moniteur,* no. 60.

was more or less identical, eliminating loges and balconies—was accompanied by close surveillance of the spectators. This was a way of acknowledging the latent power with which the public was armed. Commenting on Artaud's essay on the theater, Peter Brook speaks of a theater "in which the activity of the actor and the [activity of the] spectator are driven by the same desperate need."[26] He later adds: "This is how I understand a necessary theater; one in which there is only a practical difference between actor and audience, not a fundamental one."[27]

The theater thus contains a threatening force in the place of its spectacle, in its audience, in the space and time of its representation. Because the possibility of the "spectator being" is tied to the possibility of a subversion of the passive and alienated gaze into an active and total participation, and because an order cannot be imposed or ensured without the deferred desire for a reversal of the given order, there is present in the theater, by virtue of its constitution, a profound and secret violence. Perhaps we can in this context better appreciate Artaud's remark that

the theater like the plague is a crisis which is resolved by death or cure. And the plague is a superior disease because it is a total crisis after which nothing remains except death or an extreme purification. Similarly the theater is a disease because it is the supreme equilibrium which cannot be achieved without destruction.[28]

The question of the desired reversibility of spectator into actor—the deferred desire of the audience—applies equally to the actor and the judge. The actor is one who has successfully achieved the sender-receiver transfer; the legislator is

26. Brook, *The Empty Space*, p. 54.

27. Ibid., p. 134.

28. Antonin Artaud, *The Theater and Its Double*, trans. Mary Caroline Richards (New York: Grove Press, 1958), p. 31.

the People's Representative, one who has taken it upon himself to symbolize the public's desire to be. In his *Paradox on Acting,* Diderot wrote that a primary requirement for a great actor is that he be "a cool and calm spectator." This accounts for the dynamism inherent in the communication network described above. From this point of view, in spite of the separation of the stage and the audience, in spite of the primacy of the text, in spite of the requirements of the actor and the writer, the theater maintains a violence which is at the heart of the revolutionary process.

3

The Trial

One can imagine a history of the revolutionary tribunal that would begin with the great reform of 1791 and trace the radical modifications that transformed the practice of an equitable justice into an abusive exercise of repression—a history of a genesis followed by a decadence. The revolutionary theater seems to have followed a parallel course, marked by a series of decrees establishing freedom of spectacles and the rights of authors and actors, then gradually instituting a close surveillance that voided the content of the decrees legislated a few months earlier—a blossoming, then a dispersal of revolutionary expression.

Or, instead of a retrospective vision of a coherent genesis and a decline perceived as inevitable, one can prefer to observe those crucial moments where the system starts to give way, those instances in which the institution begins to fail, and those days that seem more full of significance not because of the consequences they entail but because of the vacancy on which they are structured. That is, for our purposes, a reflection on revolutionary law that would be determined by two acts which happened to be situated precisely *outside the law,* expressing that precarious border between the urgency of power and the necessity of law. This was the learning period in which the Assembly groped for a system that would justify putting Louis XVI on trial and, a few years later, the hour when Robespierre and twenty-one of his friends were executed without trial.

A few hours before his death, Robespierre hesitated, it is said, to sign the insurrection order that would save his life:

He took a sheet of paper, bearing the stamp of the Commune, which carried a call for insurrection already written out, and with a slow hand wrote three letters that can still be seen: R-o-b. . . . But having arrived there, his conscience protested and he threw down the pen. "Go ahead and sign it," someone said to him. — "But in whose name?"[1]

With these words Robespierre formulated one of the fundamental questions concerning the exercise of law under the Revolution and concisely recapitulated the judicial problematic that accompanied the trial of Louis XVI. Indeed, the reform of 1791 did not provide for a law that would authorize the king's arraignment. The inviolability of the monarch, preserved in the new constitution, warranted the exercise of a justice that continued to be exercised *in the name of the king*. This meant that the trial would hinge on a twofold impossibility: the impossibility of judging the only man who was by definition above the law and the impossibility of utilizing a system that was incompatible with the king's anticipated guilt. That is to say, if the king was presumed guilty—and in fact he was—the trial would create a vacancy at the summit of the very institution that made a trial possible in the first place, since justice could not be done except in the name of the king.

While various committees worked on an interpretation of the law that would enable the king to be tried, Saint-Just forcefully pointed out the incompatibility of the institution and the crime that was to be judged:

The legislative committee that spoke to you very sensibly of the vain inviolability of the king and of the maxims of eternal justice, failed to develop all the consequences of these principles, so that the draft decree that was submitted to you does not derive from them, and loses their essence, so to speak. . . . What is one to make of this last act of tyranny that would presume to be judged by the

1. Jules Michelet, *Histoire de la Révolution française,* 2 vols. (Paris: Bibliothèque de la Pléiade, 1952), 2:980.

laws it trampled on? And, Citizens, if we consented to judge him by civil action, that is, in accordance with the laws, which is to say, as a citizen, he would thereby judge us, he would judge the people themselves. For myself, I see no middle way: this man must either reign or die.[2]

D'Anglemont, executed on 20 August 1792, had, shortly before his execution, vigorously argued that the law did not represent the people but rather the king: "Do you hear the people murmuring and regretting having left it to the laws to avenge them?"[3] It was in the name of the people that the case was built and the extraordinary machine put in place that made it possible to indict Louis XVI. The fallen monarch was replaced by the notion of the sovereign people, who thereby became the basis of the law. In democratic practice, they voluntarily put the exercise of their sovereignty into the hands of their representatives. This is how a Parisian section of sans-culottes spoke of it: "If, at the very moment when the people rise up, our section comes again to address you, it is in the hope that by once again laying down its arms, by giving back the exercise of the people's sovereignty, you will make use of it for the good of the people."[4] Invested with the people's sovereignty, the Convention would have the right to judge the king.

This position, adopted in spite of Robespierre and Saint-Just, actually decreed a radical transfer of judicial power: henceforth, the name of the people took precedence over the name of the king. On another level, one might say that justice passed from the order of figuration to the order of representation. By transferring the authority of the law from the person to the group, from the Father to his children, one went from image to sign, as it were, from icon to

2. Saint-Just, *Textes choisis* (Paris: Gallimard, Idées, 1968), p. 78.

3. Albert Soboul, *Le Procès de Louis XVI* (Paris: Collection Archives Juillard, 1966), p. 14.

4. Ibid., p. 18.

abstract representation. These two orders of justice were precisely those that were lacking—one in 1792 when it was necessary to institute a law and a sovereign in order to judge the king; the other in 1794, when it was necessary to go outside the law in order to execute without trial the legitimate representatives of the people.

In the Name
of the King

"Kantorowitz," writes Michel Foucault, "gives a remarkable example of 'The King's Body'":

a double body according to the juridical theology of the Middle Ages, since it involves not only the transitory element that is born and dies, but another that remains unchanged by time and is maintained as the physical yet intangible support of the kingdom; around this duality, which was originally close to the Christological model, are organized an iconography, a political theory of monarchy, legal mechanisms that distinguish between as well as link the person of the King and the demands of the crown, and a whole ritual that reaches its height in the coronation, the funeral and the ceremonies of submission. At the opposite pole one might imagine placing the body of the condemned man; he, too, has his legal status: he gives rise to his own ceremonial and he calls forth a whole theoretical discourse. . . . In the darkest region of the political field the condemned man represents the symmetrical, inverted figure of the King.[5]

What operated in monarchical law was an order of power that was manifested by *image projection*. The ceremony of justice, and its justification, endlessly reproduced the image and the majesty of the king. To judge in the name of the king was to place the condemned in a relationship with the one

5. Michel Foucault, *Discipline and Punish,* trans. Alan Sheridan (New York: Pantheon Books, 1977), pp. 28, 29.

whom his actions had offended. Execution, says Foucault, "brought to a solemn end a war, the outcome of which was decided in advance, between the criminal and the sovereign; it had to manifest the disproportion of the power of the sovereign over those whom he had reduced to impotence."[6] The presence of the king at every stage of judicial practice was manifested in a system founded on "figuration," on the image. To judge in the name of the king was to purify the sovereign's image, which had been stained by the criminal. The king was *reproduced,* so to speak, in the victims of the criminal, and it was he who must necessarily be avenged. That the avenging of the king was also carried out in a figurative way, that is, by *reproducing* as explicitly as possible the crime that was punished, signified the closure of a judicial system that actually functioned in the name of the image and resemblance.

"Torture," Foucault continues, "correlates the type of corporeal effect, the quality, intensity, duration of pain, with the gravity of the crime, the person of the criminal, the rank of his victims." The purpose of the execution was to

pin the public torture on the crime itself; it established from one to the other a series of decipherable relations. It was an exhibition of the corpse of the condemned man at the scene of his crime, or at one of the near-by crossroads. The execution was often carried out at the very place where the crime had been committed—as in the case of the student who, in 1723, had killed several persons and for whom the presidial court of Nantes decided to set up a scaffold in front of the inn where he had committed his murders. There was the use of "symbolic" torture in which the forms of the execution referred to the nature of the crime: the tongues of blasphemers were pierced, the impure were burnt, the right hand of murderers was cut off; sometimes the condemned man was made to carry the instrument of his crime—thus Damiens was made to hold in his guilty right hand the famous dagger with which he had committed the crime, hand and dagger being smeared with sulphur and burnt

6. Ibid., p. 53.

together. As Vico remarked, this old jurisprudence was "an entire poetics." There were even some cases of an almost theatrical reproduction of the crime in the execution of the guilty man—with the same instruments, the same gestures.[7]

This justice thus appears to have been completely oriented toward punishment and execution; but it is clear that such punishment, in reproducing the crime that had been committed, in exhibiting the culpability of the condemned (public recognition of guilt), also reproduced in summary form the inquiry and the judgment. In this way each spectator was witness to the crime and to the punishment simultaneously, with the public confession of the guilty establishing the link between the two. It was indeed, as Vico said, a judicial "poetics" that was acted out up to 1791. The signs—the instruments and choice of executions—were so many motivated symbols; that is, they expressed an immediately recognizable link with the thing they represented:[8] the hand and the murder, the tongue and the blasphemy, and so on. There was a kind of cratylism of the judicial order. Between the person of the king and that of the condemned man, between the nature of the crime and that of the punishment, operated a dynamic based on mimesis. Justice projected the image of the king, and the execution that of the offense; for the spectators gathered around the scaffold, the spectacle was immediately accessible, and no ambiguity, no question must be left pending in the unfolding of the scene.

Hence, on a superficial level, to put the king on trial was to try the very person on whom the judicial system depended; on another level, it was to abolish a system of figuration that the revolution had timidly begun to throw off in 1791 by abolishing torture, by instituting a uniform death penalty (decapitation) and by simplifying the execution ritual. All these measures, it could be said, were so

7. Ibid., pp. 34, 44–45.
8. See the distinction established by C. S. Peirce, *Collected Papers,* II (Cambridge, 1932).

many steps separating the new regime from the figurative, symbolic aspect of the old judicial practice. By bringing the king to trial, the Convention confronted a last symbolic problematic: if the body of the king could become the very body of the condemned, never again would the criminal form "the symmetrical, inverted figure of the king." With the removal of the ultimate referent, the entire symbolic system collapsed. In the debates that determined the trying of the sovereign, justice was founded on a new symbolism, that of representation.

In the Name of the People

As early as 1789, in the report he presented on behalf of the committee of criminal jurisprudence, Baumetz introduced some fundamental notions: "A crime is committed: society in its entirety is injured in one of its members; hatred of crime or private interest lead to a denunciation or motivate a complaint; the Public Prosecutor is alerted by the offense or aroused by the general outcry; the crime is ascertained, pertinent facts are gathered, the traces of the crime are examined. Public order must be avenged." In the person of the victim, it is no longer the king who is offended, but society. It is not the king who demands retribution, but the people. The importance of this new element of the judicial process is such that Baumetz imagines a "general outcry," that is, one that is total, indistinct, non-individualized, demanding that the guilty be punished. The people thus summoned to participate in the revolutionary practice of justice, because they are at once the offended and the avenging parties, will have a place in the inquiry and the trial. Whereas formerly the execution alone represented the public aspect of the law, henceforth the people will be admitted to all levels of the process; the spectacle is no longer simply in the execution but in the judicial inquiry as well. Baumetz goes on to say:

"The act that demands, above all others, to be made public . . . is the report of the trial. . . . Humanity will likely urge you to remove the accused from that solemn and decisive moment, but the entire people, divided between commiseration and justice, will take care that it is done."[9]

The part here assigned to the people is of primary importance. It was a double role: the public was both assimilated to the accuser insofar as it called for revenge for a crime that had been committed against the people through one of their members, and to the accused insofar as the latter, being a member of the people as well, had a right to its sympathy and leniency. Whereas, when the king had been inviolable, there had been a heterogeneity between the one against whom the crime had been committed, the one who demanded revenge, and the one responsible for the crime, now there was an identity between the offended party and the criminal party. As we shall see, this identity was to play an important role: in 1793, this idea that the people required justice was to legitimate the trial of the king. As every crime was an offense committed not only against the person of the sovereign but quite as much against the sovereign people, the people could legitimately, by means of a simple delegation of powers, institute the tribunal that would judge the accused.

In like manner, this process instituted a number of elements characteristic of revolutionary justice which we will encounter in revolutionary theatrical practice as well.

1. Before it called for revenge, the crime demanded a judgment. Where formerly punishment, in its figurative organization, had an informative function (the nature of the crime, the confession of the guilty, hence the legitimacy of the sentence and the punishment), this information was now withdrawn from the scene of the execution and put back where it belonged, in a tribunal open to the public.

9. *Le Moniteur,* 8 October 1789, no. 69.

2. The public character of the tribunal relieved the execution of its informative function, as it were. The public, which in principle could be present at every stage of the inquiry and the judgment, had to be satisfied that justice had been rendered. Thus, the punishment was now only the last stage of a process that was open to all. The same penalty could punish the most diverse crimes without distinguishing among them; the information would be given to the public in the preliminary proceedings.

3. The execution was no longer an image, but a sign. It was no longer the figuration of the crime, nor that of the judgment; it merely signified culpability. Formerly the death penalty had contained the apology to the person of the king, the symbolic reconstitution of the injury that had been done to him, the justification of the verdict through public confession, and finally, the carrying out of justice. Revolutionary justice went from the image to the sign, from the symbolic to the arbitrary, from the figurative to the abstract, in the following manner:

First, the punishment—the death penalty, for example—was the sign that an offense had been committed; it no longer had the task of representing the crime or of symbolizing the inquiry. It abstractly signified an infraction of the law. When Chabroud proposed "that we begin by classifying the offenses, so that we may decree conjointly both the nature of the penalties and the crimes to which they will be applied,"[10] Lepelletier in protest called for a legislation of executions *independent* of the crimes they punished. Henceforth decapitation would function as a sign, that is, it would maintain a relationship of convention rather than a resemblance to the infraction it penalized.

Second, whereas formerly the judge, who was the image of the king, the supreme judge, alone decided on guilt and the penalty to be administered, now the sovereign people delegated its powers to elected judges and to jurors. This

10. *Le Moniteur,* 4 June 1791, no. 155.

delegation of powers instituted *representation* as opposed to
figuration. The jury and the judge were not the image of a
person; they were only, for the time of the trial, a temporary
authority that was borrowed from the people and would
ultimately be returned to the people.

This representation was by nature as unstable as the Revolution itself, and François Furet has explained, perhaps
better than any other historian, this ambiguity, this in-
stability of revolutionary organization. The judicial system
functioned as a language, and executions as signs; that is,
they maintained a relationship of convention with their referent (crime), a relationship that was therefore arbitrary,
whereas before 1789 the execution had maintained a symbolic
relationship with the crime, a relationship of resemblance.

This new language that formed the organizational basis of
revolutionary justice was always in a state of transformation
or, rather, displacement: "The spoken word," writes Furet,
"replaced power as the sole guarantee that power belonged
only to the people, that is, to no one in particular. And contrary to power, which was afflicted with secrecy, speech was
public and so was itself subject to the people's control."[11]
Power, and public speech, issuing from the people or from
"no one in particular," in other words, based on an abstract
notion rather than a concrete figure—governed a judicial
system that could be called "ex-centric," always in a state of
temporary or arbitrary attribution. "Since it was the people
alone who could rightfully govern, or who, being unable to
do so, must constantly reinstitute public authority, power
was in the hands of those who spoke in their name. At the
same time, this meant that power was in speaking, since
speech, being public by nature, was the instrument that
revealed what would remain hidden, hence pernicious."[12]

11. François Furet, *Penser la Révolution française* (Paris: Gallimard, 1978),
p. 72.
   12. Ibid., p. 73.

The judicial system set up during the Revolution was a system in which, through the advent of public witnesses, public accusers, public deliberations, and public sentencings, speaking played a consequential role. This open speech derived from a double failure, however—that of the king and that of the people: the failure of the king who, having betrayed the very system that he constituted, became the object of a judgment, and the failure of the people in that being a general and abstract concept, the power they had just conquered had immediately to be put back in the hands of the few.

Two systems emerge, then. The first was eloquent but practically mute: the judgment took place behind closed doors; the *lettre de cachet* (the sealed writ) placed language out of reach of a people who could not read in any case. But the spectacle of the execution, bearer of its own, figurative, language, reconveyed in its unfolding the force and majesty of justice. The second system was centered exclusively on the word and functioned as such—in a deliberate fashion, it should be added. Thus Robespierre declared to the Assembly: "You have just decided the form of consent, you are going to determine the form of proclamation; what must be established, at the same time, is the formula for it. . . . *Liberty ought to exist in the words by which you express things, and in the form of the law as in the law itself*." This concern with the *mot juste* and the definition of terms reappeared when the Convention set up the Revolutionary Tribunal, created to punish conspirators: "It is important to define what you mean by conspirator," Robespierre immediately advised.[13] The judicial discourse was closed by a single sign, the death penalty, whose function was not to reproduce crime but to signify culpability. A single penalty could sanction every crime against the nation; the accused was acquitted and released, or found guilty and executed without delay. It is

13. *Le Moniteur,* 8 October 1789, no. 69; 14 March 1793, no. 73 (my italics).

interesting to note, too, that a growing number of offenses were language or writing offenses, and a growing number of condemned individuals were language "professionals"—authors, song-writers, public orators, and so on.[14] We are here fully within a system where the signifier (the guillotine) referred to a signified (guilt) increasingly separated from its referent (the crime).

It becomes clearer what these two aspects of justice—a spectacle justice in which the punishment reproduces the crime in a figurative way, and a verbal justice in which death ratifies the sentence—have in common with the theatrical strategy, which brings together on the stage the figure and the sign, gesture and speech, the image and the symbol. "The theater, like revolutionary oratory, was assigned a quasi-legislative function," writes Peter Brooks.[15] This should be a useful viewpoint from which to examine the setting up of the Revolutionary Tribunal, by which Marat was among the first to be accused, and to study its function as an interchange in the spectacle of justice and the theater of the guillotine.

In the Name
of the Revolution

Just as it was necessary, in exceptional circumstances, to pass emergency laws, it was necessary, faced with the rise in new crimes, to institute an extraordinary Tribunal. It was voted into existence in the course of the Convention session of 10 March 1793. Article One declared:

> There shall be instituted in Paris an extraordinary criminal tribunal that will deal with every counter-revolutionary endeavor, and

14. See especially the lists of condemned men and offenses of the autumn of 1793 in *La Feuille du Salut Public*.

15. Peter Brooks, *The Melodramatic Imagination* (New Haven, Conn.: Yale University Press, 1976), p. 85.

with all attacks on the liberty, equality, unity, and indivisibility of the Republic, and with all plots tending to reestablish the royalty, or to establish any other authority attacking liberty, equality, and the sovereignty of the people, whether those accused be civil functionaries, military men, or ordinary citizens.[16]

Article Twelve added an essential clause: "The jurors shall vote aloud and shall express their declaration publicly, aloud, to the absolute majority of voting members."[17] The question of oral deliberation gave rise to long debates. During the meeting of 11 March, a deputy protested: "In decreeing that the jurors deliver their opinions aloud, you have done away with what is good in the jury institution. This manner of voting tends to interfere with their freedom and I move that this article be revoked." To this Lemarque replied: "The opinions of the previous speaker are easily reversed. You wanted to create an extraordinary tribunal; that is, a tribunal which is not bound by all the usual forms. It is only because they thought jurors would pronounce aloud that the friends of liberty have agreed that there should be jurors in this tribunal." Addressing the crucial question of the presence of a public for the judicial deliberations, he continued:

Those who say that the people of Paris might interfere with the people's delegates in their functions, insult them. There is no citizen who has not found approvers among the people when he has expressed a wish that was in accord with justice. Citizens, think back to the beginning of the revolution; the Constituent Assembly ordered the reorganization of all the government offices, and got good administrators because they had been elected by voice vote.[18]

There was now a precedent, of course, for the twofold question of speech and its audience: the king's trial. Prieur recalled the fact: "You yourselves voted aloud against the tyrant, and you were not afraid of being influenced."[19]

16. Session of 10 March 1793, *Le Moniteur,* no. 71.
17. Ibid.   18. Ibid.   19. Ibid.

On 15 March 1793, Marat declared, in terms that recalled the demonstrations that followed the decree on the freedom of theaters: "One has done nothing so long as one has not torn away the veil . . . you have wisely ordered a revolutionary tribunal to be set up; it will be the bulwark of liberty."[20] Less than a month later, Marat appeared before his judges.

The Revolutionary Tribunal was thus the result of a sort of judicial urgency whose pressure the Assembly had felt after the revolution of 10 August 1792. In the weeks that had followed, a first extraordinary tribunal had been set up because "the military court would not have been able to pronounce sentence, for no punishment exists in the military penal code for the crime of which those who took part in the plot of 10 August are accused."[21] The revolution of 10 August, the king's treason, and conspiracies against the state were all crimes which, in effect, went beyond the existing laws or judicial systems. Thus one subsequently saw the sometimes hasty setting-up of institutions created by the very crime they were devised to punish: the infraction created the law, the crime the tribunal, the accused the jury.

In this perspective, the Revolutionary Tribunal was at the same time the outcome and the failure of the judicial reform set in place in 1791: an outcome, in that its public character guaranteed judicial practice more than ever; but an admission of failure as well, since it was a matter of judging crimes that the law had not foreseen, and since it was actually the crime rather than the law that created the tribunal. This is what Danton had to say about it, on 10 March 1793:

I am aware of the importance of taking judicial measures that punish the counter-revolutionaries; for it is because of them . . . that this tribunal must take the place of the supreme tribunal of the people's vengeance. . . . Nothing is more difficult than to define a political crime. But . . . is it not necessary that extraordinary laws,

20. Session of 15 March 1793, *Le Moniteur,* no. 74.
21. Session of 15 August 1792, *Le Moniteur,* no. 231.

drawn from outside the social body, frighten the rebels and strike the guilty? Here the people's safety requires extraordinary means and terrible measures. I see no middle course between the ordinary forms and a revolutionary tribunal. [22]

This tribunal brought together—if only to abolish them—the requirements and rigors of a law that would no longer be under the authority of the Father but of the people. The tribunal operated in a judicial space whose unthinkable boundaries were established by the accused, not the judge.

Is it any wonder in this context that the act of acquittal was as strong, as eloquent as that of conviction? Here was the putting into practice, to the letter, of that revolutionary slogan printed on little tricolored posters adorning walls and shops and already vociferously proclaimed in Schiller's *Les Brigands,* the play most often performed during that period: "Liberty or death!" In any case, death became a form of purification rather than the confession of a guilt, and, like death, appearance before the tribunal became in itself a guarantee of political integrity. This was why Marat, the object of vague accusations that no one dared proclaim, demanded and obtained permission to go before the Revolutionary Tribunal. The Convention had to determine during the continuous session of 13 and 14 April if there was cause to draw up a bill of indictment. The roll-call vote gave the following results: 220 in favor, 92 against, 41 abstentions, 7 requests for adjournment. Of the 749 deputies, only 360 were present. Robespierre "contemptuously rejected" the indictment decree; Desmoulins and David voted against it as well. According to Gérard Walter:

Marat appeared to be delighted with the result. The fact of having occupied, by himself, such a long and solemn session (*before him, only Louis XVI had been honored with a roll-call vote*) filled him with pride, and he wrote on his note sheet: "What a magnificent spectacle for the enlightened observer was the session

22. *Le Moniteur,* no. 72.

of the thirteenth and fourteenth of this month. That vote will be a precious document for the history of these times."[23]

Since the matter was dragging, Marat sent a letter of protest to the National Convention and another to the Jacobins. He gave himself up—not without a certain flair—on the evening of 23 April. Delaunay wrote a bill of indictment that spoke of various infractions, including "incitement to murder and pillage" and contempt for revolutionary institutions. The report concluded: "You must show today that no one is above the law, and that if one of you is guilty, the law will be applied to him as to any other citizen."[24] Michelet describes the trial and the enthusiasm that followed the deputy's acquittal:

Marat petitioned to be tried. It was granted him, and, for the sake of form, he spent the night in prison; for his protection, several members of the Commune had themselves locked up with him. They had brought water in sealed carafes and they tasted the prison fare.

On 24 April, the day of the trial, the whole crowd from the outlying districts was on the move, agitated and fearful for the poor *Friend of the People,* cruelly hounded by the schemers, the *Statesmen.* They all shouted: "They want his life, they want to see him dead. . . . We won't stand for it."

[Marat] . . . took advantage of the occasion by reciting the story of his heroic life. . . . Nothing was left out of the comedy. All the forms were followed. The jury retired, deliberated, then, coming back in, delivered the acquittal.

"He is saved. Vive Marat!" The whole ragtag crowd went wild with happiness over his victory. . . . The women of the Halles

23. Gérard Walter, *Marat* (Paris: Albin Michel, 1933), p. 367 (emphasis mine).

24. *Rapport fait au nom du comité de législation par P. M. Delaunay le Jeune, Député du Département de Maine et Loire, Sur les délits imputés à Marat, membre de la Convention Nationale,* printed by order of the National Convention and sent to the Departments and the Armies; at Donai, by the Imprimerie de Martier, p. 13.

especially, their hearts overflowing, inundated the man and his chair with flowers, wreathing them with garlands. Marat, looking haggard, strange, lost, could scarcely be seen under that fresh spring greenery: the squalor glistened under the flowers. Delayed every minute or so by trade delegates and section orators, he went on, shaking his head with an automatic movement, responding to everything with a fixed smile resembling that of a madman. . . . It was this moment, if ever, that he hit upon the noble word he often repeated: "I made myself *anathema* for these good people of France." [25]

Michelet's description already involves an interpretation of history, of course, and in particular an interpretation of this episode as theater: the play rehearsed in advance, as it were, the spectacle of triumph, the spectators' enthusiasm—but the most interesting thing remains that word Marat used, the patriotic *anathema*. To go before the tribunal was to face excommunication in order to be reinstated; it was a kind of trial by fire. The Revolutionary Tribunal, instituted as it was around the notion of a crime that went beyond the organization of justice, implicitly assumed the guilt of the accused, so that the acquittal became the place and time of a performance every bit as spectacular as, and more extraordinary than, an execution.

The irony of this was very clear, and Marat himself had expressed it earlier: "A fine spectacle for every Frenchman, to see the citizens of Paris so respectful of the Convention that for them it is a holiday when an indicted deputy is restored to their midst!"[26] But in fact, because Marat himself demanded his trial, because he voluntarily subjected himself to the judicial process, his exoneration put him above the law. Acquitted by the Revolutionary Tribunal, owing his freedom to the same men who had ordered so many executions, he came close to the royal status of invio-

25. Michelet, *Histoire de la Révolution française,* 2:318–19.
26. Ibid., 2:321.

lability. Marat acquitted was henceforth doubly inviolable: first, because now no accusation could ever challenge his triumphal acquittal, and, second, for having—unlike the king—"earned" his inviolability by making himself anathema, outside the law, beyond or above the judicial organization. After April 1793, Marat was king. Dulaure, a journalist and political adversary of Marat at the Convention, wrote the day after the trial: " . . . the people's enthusiasm for a man . . . is the enthusiasm of slaves and not that of true republicans. When I see all the affections of a people settle on one man, lavishing tributes on him which savor of adoration, I say: these people need to idolize someone, they do not have the proud heart of a republican, they are like those who once cried *Vive le Roi*; their idolatry has merely changed objects; they have replaced one idol with another."[27] Adulated by the people, having undergone the test of the law the way one might have undergone trial by fire in the Middle Ages, Marat combined in his image the most visible attributes and the most alarming powers of the royal office. It was against a second sovereign that Charlotte Corday raised her knife; Marat's death was in a sense the second regicide of the Revolution. Just as the executed Louis XVI had been the martyr-king for the rebellious Vendée, the stabbed Marat was to become the martyr-sovereign of the Republic.

The scene of his judgment presents another aspect that should not be disregarded. Like the death sentence in times past, the acquittal gave rise to a kind of public celebration, a parade that recalls the condemned man's cart-ride to the scaffold; it was a triumph every detail of which is reencountered in the "apotheoses" that concluded a number of plays dealing with Marat's death. In the text by Gassier Saint Amand:

A shower of roses fall on the body. Then sweet music is heard; Liberty descends from a cloud with Fame, who sounds the trum-

27. Cited by Gérard Walter, *Marat,* p. 385.

pet. At the sight of her, everyone kneels. Liberty pronounces the following words . . . "Marat, whom you mourn, immortal forever, will this day share Brutus's glory." After this monologue, Liberty places a crown on Marat's head; then she rises again to the heavens. Fame sounds the trumpet; someone beats the general salute.[28]

Regarding this apotheosis, one critic observed: "The ceremony that ends the play is, except for the freshness of the costumes, rather well conceived. But I would point out to the author that nothing could be more awkward, doubtless, than to entrust the role of Liberty to the actress who just came from playing that of Charlotte Corday."[29] What looked so awkward to this scrupulous critic seems to be charged with that same fatality that, in the tribunal, closely associated death and liberty. Through her crime, Charlotte assured Marat of a liberty even more complete than that granted by the acquittal he had obtained by making himself "anathema." Now the memory of Marat would remain forever inviolable. Death became an absolute guarantee of the revolutionary purity of the People's Friend. The guilt-acquittal, condemned-revived reversal functioned on the stage as it did at the tribunal.

One sees the extent to which the Revolutionary Tribunal did for Marat what no political security could have achieved, short of assassination: by finding him not guilty, it invested him with a unique status, the status of an unassailable political force. In a sense, Marat's triumphal acquittal, like his self-induced indictment, nullified the function of the Revolutionary Tribunal, which was not, as in ordinary courts, to establish innocence or guilt but, rather, according to the terms of its constitution, to search out, identify, bring to trial, and punish the criminal par excellence, the counter-revolutionary. In this perspective, the establishing and proclaiming of innocence should not, in theory, be the product

28. Gassier Saint Amand, *La Mort de Marat.*
29. *Journal des Spectacles,* 10 August 1793, no. 41.

of criminal proceedings. Doubtless the law concerning sus-
pects passed a few weeks later indicates that in 1793 every
person without exception was liable to be accused; it nonetheless remains true that when Marat forced the tribunal to
prove his innocence, he diverted it from the function for
which it was designed. He thus neutralized, by the proclamation of his revolutionary fidelity, the implicit aim of the
revolutionary strategy. Perhaps this is why it does not seem
that Marat's innocence ought to be interpreted as a compli-
ance with a system of law but, rather, as the voluntary
indictee putting himself above the law.

   This extraordinary tribunal was conceived as the place
where, for the first time, the people would judge; it was in
fact the first institution created after the monarch's death.
The king was gone and a whole image complex collapsed
with him, giving place to a system in which the order of
resemblance, which ensured the link between the inquiry,
the crime, and the sentence, yielded to the order of representation. The judge and jurors no longer derived their authority from an inviolable sovereign but from a people who
were at once subject to the law and above the law in that
moment when they brought justice to bear, delegating their
powers to the magistrates. Hence the ambiguity of the public's presence: a public that represented the highest authority, in whose name justice was exercised, a public whom the
criminal wronged; but also a public that participated in the
accusation brought before it, that recognized itself in the
accused, that could feel every conviction as being to some
extent its own. The inviolability of the king made it possible
for justice to owe its authority to a power that was above the
law. The new tribunal founded an order in which justice
emanated from the very one whom it might at any moment
condemn.

   Hence the principle of a reversibility that had not been
possible before the king's arraignment and that more closely
established the connection with the theatrical stage.
But the spectator–actor reversibility was a constant of every

public spectacle, whereas the judge-accused reversibility—implied in the fact that the accused and the judge participated in the same authority—was recent and was especially conspicuous in the proceedings of the Revolutionary Tribunal. Marat's case was no doubt exceptional, but its exceptional nature was owing precisely to this endless possibility of reversals. Marat caused himself to be indicted, made himself anathema, outside the law, and lo and behold, he emerged acquitted, inviolable, and sovereign. What Marat achieved here was parallel to what Diderot's spectator accomplished when he went home and acted out the scene he had witnessed on the Grève or on the Boulevards. To be a spectator was to be waiting for the possibility to be an actor. There was no identification between the spectator and the role played by the actor; the only identification that was wanted occurred between the spectator and the actor as actor, not as a fictional character. To be a spectator at a trial was to be waiting to be a judge. Marat achieved just this when he declared himself anathema the better to be a sovereign; when, accused by the law he had defied, he was acquitted on the same principle and for all time. Marat's political gamble depended on particular circumstances, naturally—on the events of the spring of '93, the increasingly serious split between Montagnards and Girondins,[30] the need for a quick and dramatic action in the career of the *conventionnel*. The identity of the two registers of the tribunal and the theater came into play here at the level of the dynamisms that were in operation; and because these dynamisms operated in basically similar directions, it is not surprising that it was in the theater that the last act of the last judgment was performed.

It is appropriate at this point to raise a certain number of questions. First, does the possibility of a spectacle, whether

---

30. For many historians, it was on behalf of the Girondins that Charlotte Corday assassinated Marat. Cf. François Furet and Denis Richet, *La Révolution française,* (Paris: Fayard, 1973), pp. 159–253.

judicial or theatrical, necessarily involve the desire or even the possibility of a reversal of roles? I have already tried to show that the spectator's situation implied a kind of mutilation that did violence to him, a violence that could only be accepted in the actual or implicit expectation of a reversal of roles. Will it be granted that, merely by the public's access to the trial, the trial thus became a spectacle in the same way that pre-1789 theater performances or executions were spectacles? Clearly, here I am defining the notion of *spectacle* in terms of the possibility of being a spectator; but in that case, it will be said, everything is spectacle: a religious service, a sports event, a painting exhibition. It appears that this ambiguity can be resolved by examining not only the spectator's situation but the spectator function that the performance addresses.

In "The Science of the Concrete," Lévi-Strauss considers the difference between games and rituals and examines relationships of force that extend between the participants.

> Games appear to have a *disjunctive* effect; they end in the establishment of a difference between individual players or teams where originally there was no indication of inequality. And at the end of the game they are distinguished into winners and losers. Ritual, on the other hand, is the exact inverse; it *conjoins,* for it brings about a union (one might even say communion in this context) or in any case an organic relation between two initially separated groups, one ideally merging with the person of the officiant and the other with the collectivity of the faithful.[31]

The spectacle, in this perspective, is the inverse of both rituals and games. It is the activity in which every transfer of forces, every disjunctive or conjunctive dynamic, is at once the object of a desire and the object of a prohibition. The spectacle is that organization in which the activity of the

31. Claude Lévi-Strauss, *The Savage Mind* (Chicago: University of Chicago Press, 1966), p. 32.

actor (in the broadest sense) requires a spectator and excludes his participation. Without the presence of the spectator there can be no significant justice and no theater; equally, however, without his passivity there can be neither a judgment nor a performance. It is in this sense that a close connection can be established between the revolutionary tribunal as a spectacle of the people's justice and the revolutionary theater as a spectacle of the people's triumph. Just as formerly the execution had no meaning unless it was public, the tribunal had no juridical value except in the presence of the people, since only the people could guarantee its legitimacy and integrity; however, like the presence of an audience in the theater, this presence had to be the object of a strict and indefatigable surveillance.

4

The Texts

Marat was assassinated on 13 July 1793. Charlotte Corday, seeing in him "the monster" responsible for the fall of the Girondin party, had first thought of carrying out her plan in a public, spectacular fashion: she chose the date of 14 July— she would assassinate the *conventionnel* during the anniversary festival of the fall of the Bastille. When the celebration was canceled, she decided to kill Marat in the middle of the Assembly. From her prison cell she wrote to Barbaroux: "On leaving Caen, I expected to sacrifice him on the summit of the Montagne of the National Convention."[1] The ritualistic, quasi-religious character of the "sacrifice" had to be modified when Charlotte Corday learned that Marat had not appeared at the Convention for several weeks. On the morning of the 13th she bought an ebony-handled knife, and at about ten o'clock presented herself at the deputy's door. Having been refused entry, she returned in the evening, promising the People's Friend a list of deputies, traitorous to the Revolution, who were hiding out in Caen. The rest of the story is common knowledge: she stabbed Marat in the bathtub where he was treating his skin ailment. Arrested on the spot, she offered no resistance, insisted she

1. This letter is cited in most works on either Marat or Charlotte Corday. Jules Michelet also mentions it (*Histoire de la Révolution française,* 2 vols. [Paris: Bibliothèque de la Pléiade, 1952], 2:500). Barbaroux was a deputy from Marseilles and a friend of Madame Roland. After the events of 31 May 1793, he went into hiding in Normandy, where he met Charlotte Corday. Saint-Just had him declared an outlaw and a traitor to the country; he was arrested, and guillotined without a trial on 20 June 1794.

had acted alone, and was guillotined on 19 July, less than a week after her crime.

Marat's assassination provoked a popular uproar the aftereffects of which extended for many months the influence of the man whom the people had, as Dulaure put it, "idolized." Yet, in spite of this violent public reaction, or perhaps because she contrasted so strongly with it, the calm and tranquillity of the assassin impressed the judge and the public. Even the newspapers did not hesitate to express their admiration. This is how *Le Moniteur* of 29 July described the execution (italics mine):

> Going to the scaffold, Marie Corday heard nothing but applause and bravos along the way. A smile was the only sign by which she showed any emotions. When she had mounted on to *the theater of her agony,* her face still had the freshness and color of a contented woman. The fatal blade sliced off her head. A certain Legros, after having seized it to show it to the people, gave it several slaps. This despicable act caused the people to murmur, and it was punished by the police court.[2]

La Chronique de Paris was just as unsparing of its admiration for the courage and strength of the young woman; moreover, these newspapers were simply recording the admiration of the same people who had so violently mourned Marat's death. Once again we encounter, in connection with the theater of justice, the apparent inconsistency of a public captivated both by the victim and by the executioner,

2. Michelet's account is not without interest:

> When the executioner snatched away her shawl, the young girl in her, her modesty offended, reappeared; she hurried forward to meet her death. When her head fell into the basket, one of Marat's followers, a carpenter who helped out the executioner, ran his knife up the severed neck and held the head aloft to show it to the crowd; a base frenzy made him strike it with his hand, and a tremor of horror ran through the murmuring crowd. The head seemed to blush. It was probably a perfectly ordinary optical illusion: the crowd was bewildered; the red of the sun crowded through the leafy trees along

acclaiming in a single cry the assassinated hero and the hand that had struck him down. However, this contradiction dissolves when we consider the people in their spectator function. It is not surprising that a double cult came out of this sacrifice, two images that are not opposed to one another like those of liberty and oppression, the martyr and the murderer, but form parallel figures of the Revolution, both outside the law, both fiercely devoted to republican virtues.

The murder had first been conceived as a public act, but if the assassination in fact took place in the noiseless calm of Marat's apartment, nonetheless the theater soon took charge of the event, profoundly altering the facts and political appearances. Three days after Marat's death, the *Journal des Spectacles* published the following letter:

Paris, 14 July, Year II of the French Revolution, at three o'clock in the afternoon.

Citizen, a cruel event has transpired, saddening the hearts of true republicans. Marat has been assassinated, and the traitors he denounced exist! . . . the perfidious monsters, the infamous partisans of moderatism, the friends of the laws who had tried to portray him as a bloodthirsty tiger, because he wanted to stop the spilling of patriots' blood, which has flowed in torrents, by causing the heads of conspirators to fall under the blade of justice; these monsters, I say, take pleasure in devouring my unhappy country. My heart, all aflame, will lead public opinion against them, and my body offers itself to the blows of the assassins.

---

the Champs-Elysées and shone in its eyes. Public opinion was satisfied when the Paris Commune and the Tribunal put the man into prison.

(*History of the French Revolution,* trans.
Keith Botsford, vols. 4, 6, and 7,
Wynnewood, Pa.: Livingston Publishing
Company, 1973, 6:146)

Here one may already note a properly romantic view of the revolutionary heroine.

I wrote a drama entitled *L'Ami du Peuple ou les intrigans démasqués* [*The People's Friend, or the Schemers Unmasked*]; my play, finished two months ago, has been for eight days in the hands of Citizen Monvel, whom I asked to represent it before the administration of the Theater of the Republic. One sees that I did not await the heartrending situation that afflicts us in order to reveal and deliver to infamy the odious schemes of the so-called friends of the laws, who preach peace and cut your throats; and if my play had been presented sooner, perhaps we would not have had to regret one of the most courageous defenders of political equality.[3]

This hasty letter is a particularly revolutionary text, addressed to the public: a public in the singular, as is shown by the interpellation *"citoyen," "toi," "ami de la République,"* as opposed to the plural used for the traitors and conspirators. Once again one hears the echo of the pronoun *tu* of classical tragedy, of the Roman model, and the *vous,* the imprecise and threatening plurality of the Court, the moderates, the enemies. Much could be said concerning the function of "conspirators"—that group, uncertain in number, whose activity was a constant menace to the sober republican "singularity." A paradox: royal absolutism engendered the *je* of absolute authority and the *vous,* the *ils* of treason, whereas democracy addressed in the singular the people it governed and represented. This letter, with its dramatic tone, was also theatrical. As Roland Barthes says, concerning revolutionary language, "truth, through the bloodshed that it costs, becomes so weighty that its expression demands the very forms of theatrical amplification."[4]

The author of the letter, Camaille Saint-Aubin, who was an actor in the Théâtre de l'Ambigu-Comique, saw the

3. *Journal des Spectacles,* 16 July 1793, no. 16.

4. Roland Barthes, *Writing Degree Zero,* trans. Annette Lavers and Colin Smith (New York: Hill and Wang, 1968), p. 21. Regarding the revolutionary *tutoiement,* I would call attention to the play by Aristide Valcour, *Le Vous et le toi,* performed in November 1793 at the theater of the Cités-Variétés. Another play, *La Plus parfaite égalité ou le tu et le toi,* by Dorvigny, was presented in December 1793 at the Théâtre National. In it one finds this

opening of his play on 6 September at the Théâtre du Palais-Variétés. "The play is a success," said the *Journal des Spectacles* of 8 September. It was presented regularly in September, October, and November—a respectable success.[5] This "comedy" has a cast of characters that includes Doucemont, a merchant, his daughter Lucille, and Démophile (Marat), a municipal officer in the Commission des Subsistances.[6] Démophile is accused of treason by Forcerame (Rolland) and Caesaret (Dumouriez). Like Marat before the Revolutionary Tribunal, Démophile triumphs over his accusers and, while the people acclaim him, he narrowly escapes from an assassination attempt. The play ends with this verse:

> Tout un peuple l'acclame et l'appelle son père.
> An entire people acclaim him and call him their father.

As inoffensive as it appears, this play quickly gave rise to a rather interesting polemic. The *Journal des Spectacles* published on 7 Frimaire a new article on the play by Camaille Saint-Aubin: "*L'Ami du Peuple,* a three-act comedy in verses, which we reviewed previously, and which obtained so much success at the Théâtre du Palais-Variétés, was not so fortunate in Marseilles at the Théâtre Pelletier, where it played for the first time on Quintidi 5 Brumaire." There

---

declaration: "Oh! the splendid news! No more *vous*! By correcting this abuse of language the ties of fraternity are drawn closer, and the aristocracy is sought out in its last positions" (quoted by E. Jauffret, *Le Théâtre révolutionnaire,* Paris: Furne, Jouvet, 1869, p.269).

5. From 6 through 10 September; revived 18, 21, 26, 29, and 30 September and 12 October. It was performed on 23 October at the Théâtre de l'Ambigu-Comique and revived at the Théâtre du Palais-Variétés on 24, 26, and 30 October. A play also entitled *L'Ami du peuple,* presented on 28 Brumaire and 2 and 3 Frimaire at the Cité-Variétés, was very probably that of Gassier Saint Amand, published in Paris by Maradan in 1793.

6. TRANSLATOR'S NOTE: The Commission des Subsistances was "a body which enjoyed the most extensive powers and which had overall control of production, trading conditions, and transportation" (Albert Soboul, *The French Revolution 1787–1799,* New York: Vintage Books, 1974, p. 344).

followed a harsh review by a "Paris Jacobin" named La-croix, and then a decree:

> On behalf of the Republic, the representatives of the people for the departments and armies of the Midi—considering that *L'Ami du Peuple,* a charming but no less fraudulent title, is a Feuillant play all the more apt to lead public opinion astray as the play's interest is adroitly directed toward a merchant, that is, a man of that class which in Marseilles employed its treasures to bankroll the counter-revolution; considering that the subject of this work only tends to dull the just suspicions of the people toward the hypocrites who call themselves friends, and to have the people associate the main character with those merchants who, in order to attach the people to themselves, caused bread to be put back to five pennies during the time of the section system—do decree that perform-ances of the play called *L'Ami du Peuple* shall not take place from this day on, and that it shall be removed from the repertory.[7]

L'Ami du Peuple was presented by its author as a reply to *L'Ami des Lois;* he alludes, of course, to Laya's cele-brated play that momentarily interrupted the king's trial.[8] In a more general sense, the play clearly opposes love of the people to love of the laws. This is again the echo of Marat anathematized, an outlaw, a renegade, a regicide, and a king all in one, through his love for the fatherland, hence for the people.

7. *Journal des Spectacles,* 7 Frimaire, no. 148.

8. Laya's *L'Ami des lois* was one of the most controversial plays of the Revolution, and the story of its performances is given a good deal of space in all works on the revolutionary theater. I will only cite comments by E. Jauffret:

> During the month of January (1793) an extraordinary agitation held sway in Paris. The center of this agitation was, on the one hand, at the Convention, where Louis XVI's case was being tried, and on the other hand, at the Comédie Française, where *L'Ami des lois,* a verse comedy in five acts, by Citizen Laya was being performed. . . . If *L'Ami des lois* had only been an anti-revolutionary play, it would

This exclusion of the law on behalf of a form of paternity—which is not unconnected with the monarchical structure—was also at the center of the polemic that censored the play: could one represent Marat as a merchant, or as a personage associated with a merchant? Could Marat belong to the Commission des Subsistances? The merchant was the monopolist, of course, and hence the counter-revolutionary, but the bread image also suggests the figure of the father-provider or foster-father. Now, the foster-father was the father of monarchical law, the king—one is reminded of the march of the women on Versailles in the first days of the Revolution, demanding bread for their families. Here one of the basic paradoxes of the paternal function in revolutionary imagery is established; namely, that legal paternity excluded real paternity. The law was the falsification of the role; one was not a father by right, but by the heart. Démophile/Marat expressed this forcefully: "Les lois! quel nom sacré! mais quel piège odieux!" ["The laws! what a sacred word! but what a hateful trap!"] (II, 4).

This paradox was taken up again in a play written after Saint-Aubin's comedy but performed before it, opening on 8 August 1793 at the Théâtre des Variétés Amusantes. *L'Ami du Peuple, ou la mort de Marat* [*The People's Friend, or the Death of Marat*], written by Gassier Saint Amand, was an historical piece in one act, followed by a funeral ceremony.

---

have gone unnoticed or would have made only a small stir; but it had a quite different significance. The author had in fact set out to tear the mask from the political schemers, from that abominable faction whose power was based on thievery, murder, and terror.

(E. Jauffret, *Le Théâtre révolutionnaire*,
pp. 203–4)

Marat was recognized in the play as the character Duricrane. The content of this play and the disturbances that accompanied the performances were the subject of a discussion in the Convention on the very day the king's death was to be voted (cf. above, ch. 1).

The critic of the *Journal des Spectacles* found much to criti-
cize in the play: "An historical incident does not always
suffice as the subject of a play. . . . The author has made just
about all he could of the event. But should one allow himself
to show indignant spectators an action as revolting as an
assassination? No, not unless the criminal expires as soon as
the awful deed is done."[9] It may seem surprising that the
critic should be apprehensive about seeing on stage a punishment that the people witnessed every day in the public
square. Yet, under the cover of propriety, he formulates a
basic problematic of representation and the secret violence
that accompanies it, a point to which we shall return; he also
evokes—once more—what might be considered another
defect of the law: could one represent Marat's death without
representing the death of Charlotte Corday?

We shall see later that these two deaths are incompatible
and that, in order to be staged, the death of Marat has to
leave the crime unpunished, the punishment suspended, the
event incomplete. What immediately appears is, rather,
Marat's "resurrection." In a sense, the assassination remains
"outside the law"; more than an infraction, it is the
confirmation of the exceptional destiny of the People's
Friend. In this perspective, the punishment adds nothing,
cannot add anything to the death of the *conventionnel*, which
he almost wished for. Sacrifice does not call for vengeance;
the offering of life is an act of peace. *Marat was not assassinated; he gave* his life: "What does life matter to me if I
manage to consolidate the happiness of the Republic? Do I
not owe myself body and soul to my country?" and further
on: "When I shall have to lose my life, no sacrifice will be
too great in order to merit that confidence of which I am so
proud. Labor, sleep, repose, I sacrifice all, and if my blood
can serve to cement the peace and well-being of my fellow
citizens, I am ready to shed it" (scene 4). Before he died,
Marat married—extra-legally, before Nature alone—Citi-

9. *Journal des Spectacles,* 10 August 1793, no. 20.

zen Evrard. Charlotte herself strangely resembled her victim, in offering her life to the country before committing her murder.

The play ends with an appeal to the people: "We all lose a *father,* a friend. Let us pay to his memory the honors that are his due, and never forget that the hearts of all French people are the Pantheon where the people's friend must live on" (scene 13; my italics). There follows an apotheosis in which Marat's name is "placed in the Temple of Memory next to that of Brutus."

Another play inspired by Marat was performed for the first time on 16 Brumaire, Year II (6 November 1793) at the Opéra-Comique National. It had nine consecutive performances and was taken up again on 28 Brumaire, and 24 Frimaire, and 5, 6, and 14 Nivôse—for that period, something of a success. The play, by Citizen Mathelin, was entitled *Marat dans le souterrain des Cordeliers ou la journée du 10 août* [*Marat in the caves of the Cordeliers, or the Day of 10 August*].[10] The review in the *Journal des Spectacles* was laudatory: "This play is very pleasantly written, and the patriotic feelings that guided the author speak sufficiently well of him. At the end of the performance, the author's presence was demanded with great cries; he appeared and was loudly applauded."[11] *La Feuille du Salut Public* on the same day published a favorable report, which was qualified, however, by reservations having to do mainly with the question of power and the law:

An historical prose piece in two acts, presented the day before yesterday at this theater, was enthusiastically received. . . . I have essentially two observations to make to Citizen Mathelin, the author of this work, which does honor to his patriotism and his literary talent. Ambroise several times calls Marat his master. Now, if he had been a domestic in the extension one gave to the word then, it is a sure thing that he would not have allowed a man

10. The play was published in Paris by Maradan in 1793.
11. *Journal des Spectacles,* 18 Brumaire, Year II (8 November 1793), no. 129.

to acknowledge him as his master. A citizen has no other master than the law, and Marat knew this before a decree taught it to those who must be taught how to be a man.

When the good sans-culotte comes to ask Marat for the guidance that the people had to have during the day of 10 August, Marat does not give an affirmative reply, he speaks of prudence and respect for the laws. The moment was decisive and Marat's replies are not. Doubtless there is some truth in allowing the people the merit of energy; but the people don't say: "Marat, give us energy," they request Marat to guide them; consequently, the latter should reply as a man instructed in the crimes of the court, and persuaded, as he was, that the first of all the laws is the safety of the people and the fall of the tyrants.[12]

This paradox on the right exercise of the law was directed at a text about which Mathelin wrote: "My sole aim was to bring back to life the memory of a man dear to the entire nation."[13] The play is a rather free depiction of a "death" of Marat followed by a glorious resurrection. Marat has taken refuge in the caves of the monastery of the Cordeliers, pursued by the aristocrats and other enemies who have sworn to kill him. It is 10 August 1792. At midnight (opening of the second act) the alarm bell rings, and when dawn appears, Marat emerges from the underground in order to hail the Revolution, which he has been able to lead from his "tomb." The metaphor underlies the whole organization of the play. The deputy chooses to "bury himself alive" in the caves of the monastery where the past crimes of the "robed charlatans" are evoked. The "redoubt at best fit for containing the dead" opens triumphantly at the end of the play, and the last words of the text are those of the crowd carrying the revolutionary who was delivered up from the darkness: *"Long live* our friend, *long live* Marat!"

12. *La Feuille du Salut Public,* 18 Brumaire, Year II, no. 130.
13. Preface to *Marat dans le souterrain des Cordeliers.*

Marat plays a passive role here, and one could interpret this play as a ritual of resurrection instead of as a token of admiration for the martyr of the Republic. Yet, as *La Feuille du Salut Public* pointed out, in this simple ceremonial there returns, in a familiar and obsessive way, the never-resolved link between law and necessity. Marat was not a master, but didn't the situation call for action outside the law? And the revolutionary theater never stopped questioning this father without children, this king without investiture.

A last play, performed for the first time on 3 February 1794, pointedly reaffirms the notion that staging Marat's death meant tirelessly repeating the rites of sacrifice and resurrection. Entitled *La Mort de Marat,* [14] the text bears this epigraph: "Let them fear him still, he will live again in us." In this cautionary notice, one reencounters the imprecise plural of treason, the mark of the conspirators; Marat vows to fight against them, and, once again, gives his life for the welfare of the people. Here Charlotte Corday briefly explains the reasons for her action. They are not political but personal: she will avenge her father and her lover by a single action. Shortly before his death, Marat utters the following:

> Ami, reviens au peuple, et dis-lui que j'espère,
> Au salut de l'Etat veiller encor longtemps.
> Le soin de son bonheur remplit tous mes instants;
> Il fixe tous mes voeux, il est ma loi suprême:
> Heureux si tout entier, à ce peuple que j'aime,
> Je pouvais, de la mort brisant les tristes fers,
> Eterniser des jours qu'il m'a rendu si chers.
>
> *(II, 2)*

Friend, go back to the people, and tell them I expect to attend to the safety of the state for a long time still. My every moment is

14. This play was first performed in Toulouse, at the Théâtre de la République. It was printed in Lyons by the Imprimerie des Droits de l'Homme and published by the Républicain Français, rue des Sans-Culottes, Year III of the Republic.

filled with concern for their welfare; it rules my desires, it is my supreme law. How happy I would be if, for that people I love, I could break death's woeful grip and fully eternalize the days they rendered so dear to me.

The apotheosis, presented after the tragedy, represents a public square. Marat's body is brought and respectfully placed in the shade of the Tree of Liberty. A citizen evokes his memory:

> Marat, dans la nuit des tombeaux,
> Remportera sur eux des triomphes nouveaux:
> Son nom, des citoyens, ornera la banière,
> Et poursuivra le crime à son dernier repaire.
> Vivant, ils le craignaient, mort, ils bravent ses coups:
> Qu'ils le craignent encor, il va revivre en nous. . . .
> De ton civisme en nous éternise les feux,
> Revis pour ta Patrie, et veille encor pour elle.

Marat, in the night of the tombs, will win new triumphs over them: his name will embellish the citizens' banner and will pursue crime to its last haunt. Living, they feared him; dead, they defy his blows; let them fear him still, he will live again in us. . . . Eternalize the fires of your patriotism in us, live again for your country, and watch over her still.

One sees how insistently, in these modest homages to the assassinated regicide, the themes of paternity and the law keep returning, mixed with a resurrectional metaphor: the people have lost a father, a father who had no other law but his love for the people; or again, the people have lost Marat, and because Marat never had any other law than his love for the people, his death confirms his paternity.

Naive in their expression, elementary in their rhetoric, these texts reassert the impossibility of forgetting. Curiously, it is not so much that Marat's distinctive individuality defies death, as that a persistent danger threatens the people. So long as there are "traitors," so long as there are violations of the law, the memory of Marat will live on. However, far from being a judicial exercise that would condemn the murderer, that would dishonor the name Charlotte Corday for all time, these plays take almost no interest in the fate of the assassin. They obliterate death, and celebrate continuity. In this perspective, it is clear that these texts are not very different from the tradition that when a king died, one cried: "The king is dead, long live the king!" for one knew very well that the king could not die, that the heir maintained the slender and implacable thread of the reigning genealogy; the transmission of power was immediate, the inheritance uncontested, the paternal status always maintained. In the framework of the Revolution, which had taken care to judge Louis XVI as the *last* of the kings and which had successfully staged a drama entitled *The Last Judgment of the Kings,* [15] there was a rupture and a discontinuity: no inheritance could be counted on, no transmission was possible: the father had children but no heirs. With Marat assassinated, there was simply a blotting out of the crime. One had to cry: "Marat is dead, long live Marat!"

Actually, the murder needs to be re-examined from the viewpoint, not of the victim, but of the assassin. For Marat, the important thing was to die, and we have seen that this death was foreseen, accepted, desired; for the assassin, it was a matter of justifying the crime. As to the trial and execution of the king, the full responsibility lay entirely with the regicides. The real death of Marat was to be staged, therefore, in the theatrical works devoted to the memory of Charlotte Corday.

In the years that followed, there were three plays earnestly dedicated to the assassin of Jean-Paul Marat: *Charlotte*

15. This play, by Sylvain Maréchal, was presented for the first time on 18 October 1793 at the Théâtre de la rue de Richelieu. It was an overwhelming success. Cf. Daniel Hamiche's study in *Le Théâtre et la Révolution* (Paris: Union Générale d'Editions, 1973), pp. 171–94.

Corday by Jean–Baptiste Salles, *Charlotte Corday,* an anonymous tragedy dated 1795, and *Charlotte Corday, or the Modern Judith,* also anonymous, dated 1797.[16] These plays no doubt had only a limited audience, despite the political changes that had resulted from the fall of Robespierre. They are nonetheless interesting for the strange resemblance they show to the texts that eulogized Marat: the same language, at once pompous and naive, the same praises, the same fervor. The three plays deliberately ignore the historical facts. In the first, Charlotte Corday is, rather implausibly, the mistress of the deputy Hérault de Séchelles. In the second, the assassination takes place just where Charlotte had wished it to take place, in the middle of the Convention, and on the symbolic date of 31 May 1793, the day of the fall of the Girondins. And in the last play, Charlotte Corday escapes from the guillotine and marries her rescuer, a royalist officer.

The anonymous author of the second tragedy prefaces his play with a classic interpretation of the circumstances that led ineluctably to the death of the People's Friend. Girondist in inspiration, this preface vigorously denounces the abuses of the Montagne and attempts to show how the latter had begun to betray the Revolution when Marat was assassinated:

> Without warning, the notorious conspiracy of 31 March 1793 came to rob the world of the fruit of two great revolutions. It overthrew the party of the Gironde, or to be more exact, all Frenchmen who wanted the Republic and laws, and enthroned Marat, Hébert, Danton, Robespierre, and the whole faction of Jacobins of those days, composed of men who were perverse, ambitious, bloodthirsty, and, almost all of them, wretched.
>
> . . . *Marat reigned at last.* He was the first tyrant of France in those times of anarchy: he was the only one for whom altars have been

16. The text of the tragedy by Salles was reprinted in Paris, by Miard, in 1864; the quotations here are from that edition. The text of the second tragedy is dated 1795 and does not carry the name of a printer. The last tragedy only bears the mention Caen 1797.

erected, altars that will one day be shattered. He would have died on the scaffold like his successors, if the department of Calvados had not included in its precincts the most intrepid republican that has ever existed. . . . Charlotte Corday in her prime conceived the sublime purpose of laying down her life for the country and of ridding it of the basest of tyrants. The calumny that feels the need to spread its venom over all the virtues and to tarnish the luster of the finest of actions has spread it abroad that royal fanaticism and the desire to avenge a lover, whose death was attributed to Marat, had inspired this heroic woman. Vile slanderers, hold your tongues and respect Charlotte: love of country and liberty, hatred of tyrants—these are the sentiments that inflamed and consumed her being.[17]

These lines situate rather well the feeling that venerated the extraordinary assassin. It was not so different, in its formulation, from the admiration that surrounded the People's Friend: for the spectator of those great days of the Revolution, Marat and his assassin had the same sober determination, the same patriotism, and that same disregard for the laws which, in both cases, was to decide their deaths. The two images resemble one another—irreconcilable, at once close and alien, both obsessed by the vision of an exceptional destiny.

The first tragedy was written even before Charlotte Corday's execution, by Jean-Baptiste Salles, a deputy from the Gironde who had been in hiding since the famous *journée* of 31 May 1793.[18] The play was to be performed in prisons. The action takes place in Paris, where the members of the Committee of Public Safety consult together and become alarmed over their own crimes. This scene calls to mind the notorious "public confession" of condemned men of former times. Once again, and in a much more clear-cut

17. Op. cit., p. 9 (emphasis mine).
18. Salles, friend of Barbaroux and likewise proscribed after the fall of the Girondin party, was arrested and executed in Bordeaux on 17 June 1794.

way than in the plays glorifying Marat, the theater recapitulated the judicial structure. Hérault de Séchelles describes
the atrocities committed by the Jacobin party and lingers
over the role of Marat:

> Marat, l'affreux Marat, à nous-même en horreur,
> Partout pour nous servir, a soufflé sa fureur,
> Commandé les soupçons, les haines, la vengeance,
> Et notre politique a dévasté la France.
>
> (I, 1)

Marat, the dreadful Marat, everywhere to serve us, has breathed
his fury on us, horror-struck, has commanded suspicion, hatred,
vengeance, and our policy has devastated France.

Hérault de Séchelles fearfully predicts that one day a vir-
tuous assassin will come and put an end to these abuses.
Danton's rejoinder is significant:

> Quoi, ces vaines terreurs troublent vos espérances!
> Où est donc ce Brutus?
>
> (I, 1)

What, these vain terrors trouble your expectations! Then where
is this Brutus?

Henriot abruptly interrupts the meeting and tells of the
assassination of Marat, which he himself witnessed (thus
underscoring the necessarily public aspect of a truly revolutionary justice). Robespierre, already perceived as the Committee's strategist, intervenes:

> Plus de délais, frappons! A ce peuple éperdu
> Montrons ce corps sanglant, attisons sa colère;
> Disons qu'il est trahi, qu'il vient de perdre un père.
>
> (I, 4)

No more delays, it is time to strike! Let us show these bewil-
dered people the bloodstained body, let us stir up their anger. We

shall say that they have been betrayed, that they have just lost a father.

The act ends on these words by Danton:

> Si l'effroi fait trembler, c'est sur un tribunal.
> Désormais ne frappons que d'un glaive légal.
>
> (I, 4)

Where terror makes people tremble is at the tribunal. Henceforth, let us strike only with a legal blade.

The second act represents the tribunal, where Charlotte Corday intimidates her accusers by her composure and her tranquil virtue. Robespierre is furious, Danton undecided, and Hérault de Séchelles captivated. Returning to the public confession of the first act, he acknowledges Marat's guilt:

> Je sais trop que Marat fut un traître;
> Je déteste ce monstre; et, mieux que toi, peut-être
> De tous ces noirs complots je ressens les effets.
> Ami! c'est aujourd'hui surtout que je le hais:
> Il est mort. Et quel sang va couler sur sa tombe!
>
> (III, 1)

I know all too well that Marat was a traitor; I detest that monster; and more than you, perhaps, I feel the effects of those evil plots. Friend! Today, above all, I hate him: he is dead. And to think of the blood that is going to flow over his tomb!

With Marat guilty, Charlotte Corday is innocent. The assassination is no longer a crime but a sentence; justice is done. Hérault goes on to praise the assassin:

> Ton triomphe sera la mort des oppresseurs
> . . . leur vengeance
> Fonde un culte à Marat et subjugue la France.
> Non, lâches! ce beau sang ne sera pas versé.
> De nos droits reconquis le règne est commencé,

> Elle vivra. Son nom, comme un signal de gloire,
> Va marcher devant nous et fixer la victoire,
> Et nos cris triomphants, honorant ses vertus,
> Vont la nommer partout plus grande que Brutus.
>
> (IV, 3)

Your triumph will be the death of the oppressors . . . their vengeance founds a cult to Marat and subjugates France. No, cowards! this fair blood shall not be spilled. The reign of our reconquered rights has begun, she will live. Her name, like a signal of glory, will march in front of us and secure the victory, and our triumphant cries, honoring her virtues, will everywhere call her greater than Brutus.

Hérault de Séchelles dies poisoned before he is able to defend the young woman, and the play ends with Charlotte's execution—she, too, a martyr of the Republic. The reference to Brutus in these eulogies, which once again draw together the assassin and her victim, should no longer surprise us; in his apotheosis, Marat sits beside Brutus, the two united by their fight against the tyrants; they both represent the highest virtue. Charlotte Corday, also a regicide, joins Brutus in posterity. The formula immediately circulated among the outlawed Girondins. In a letter he wrote to Jean-Baptiste Salles toward the end of the year 1793, Barbaroux remarked: "My friend, so your memory has not recalled to you all the circumstances of the death of Charlotte Corday? How is it you have not portrayed on the stage that interesting Adam Lux, deputy from Mayence, one truly enamored of Charlotte, and who, for her, for writing a text in which he painted her *greater than Brutus,* got himself locked up in the Abbaye?"[19] Reunited in death and in posterity, the assassin and her victim both laid claim to the glory of Brutus; as we shall see, this involved a symbolism that went far beyond regicide, recalling that the Revolution was childless.

19. This letter was published with the text of the tragedy, p. 159.

The action of the second tragedy, written after the trial and execution of Charlotte, takes place, the author tells us, on 31 May 1793 because "by this means, I had the occasion to sketch that disastrous day, which changed free France into a *theater* of murders and banditry."[20] History became theater and theater became history. There are other documents placed before the beginning of the tragedy: extracts from the trial proceedings, the letter the murderess wrote to Barbaroux on 16 July 1793,[21] in which she says simply: "People are less than content to have but a woman of no consequence to offer to the spirit of a great man." Once more a sacrifice, a funeral ritual, where Marat acts the part of the merciless idol. At the Palais Royal, when Charlotte hears of the fall of the Girondins, she cries out:

> O Ciel! Marat l'emporte, et le peuple égaré,
> Tombe sans doute aux pieds de ce monstre adoré!
>
> (I, 3)

Heavens! Marat triumphs, and the misguided people doubtless are falling at the feet of that beloved monster!

The second act takes place at the National Convention; the statue representing Liberty is covered by a veil; like a ghost, she silently presides over the deliberations of a Convention at once deranged by its wrath and determined by its implacable rhetoric. Not surprisingly, Robespierre speaks of justice. "The people were born to believe, not to judge," he says. "For them punishment is proof of the crime." Thus expressing what had for many years ensured the power and the conviction of public executions in their complex ceremonial and in the rigidity of a system sustained by a king, he demands new victims. Marat, justifying the execution that is going to take place, speaks, as though in a trance, of his "cold cruelty."

20. Op. cit., p. 9 (my italics).
21. Cf. footnote 1, p. 71.

> Un sentiment nouveau me saisit, me transporte,
> Et d'un pouvoir terrible à peine suis-je armé,
> Que de meurtre et de sang je me sens affamé.
>
> (II, 6)

A new feeling takes hold of me, transports me, and with a terrible power no sooner am I armed than I feel starved for blood and murder.

Shortly afterward, Charlotte stabs him. He dies, but not without having time to repent, in a final reconciliation at the gates of exile and posterity.

The last act represents a prison where Charlotte Corday waits courageously for death. Like Marat (the theatrical figure) before her, she desires this sacrifice which will forever bear witness to her Republican virtue: "Without terror, I abandon life: how sweet dying is to me, dying for my country!" (III, 1). The tragedy ends with the accused woman's departure for the guillotine.

This text, while it takes liberties with history, speaks plainly of Marat's death; that is, it states his irrevocable end, it recapitulates and summarizes the judicial proceeding which was the only means, in those times, to close a disquieting tomb. The play "does justice" to the virtues of the assassin. In it the great auditorium of the Convention is arranged like a theater, clearly evoking the memory of the staging of the great judgment, that of the "last of the kings." It presents a confession by the condemned, a public proclamation of the crimes of Marat, who deliriously describes the intoxication of power and the trances of cruelty on a throne he had usurped such a short time before.

In this perspective, Charlotte Corday again commits no crime; she is justice done in the name of the people. If Marat is dead, the play clearly says, it is from having wanted to reign. The Revolution legitimated the first regicide; it was important that it rehabilitate the second. Charlotte certainly does not avenge Louis XVI, but under that law which allowed his execution, she pushes republican rigor to the ex-

treme. What the theater says here is that Marat's death constitutes the second regicide of the Revolution, and that
without this inexorable event, the Revolution could not
have continued to be. In this sense, one sees what Charlotte
Corday the theatrical figure conveys that is properly tragic.
Whereas Marat lives on indefinitely in the memory of the
people, Corday is the heroine of a necessary and useless
gesture; it is she who guarantees that virtue will triumph,
while her death announces that it was already too late.

Charlotte Corday ou la Judith moderne [*Charlotte Corday or
the Modern Judith*], published in 1797, is royalist in its political outlook, and it is not known whether the text was ever
staged. Its only interest for us is its repeated justification of
the assassination, which is presented as a crime of war and as
the just reward for a monstrous course of action which
Marat himself admits to the public before his death.[22]

What we are left to consider, then, is that in the theatrical
enclosure Marat and Charlotte Corday meet again in an
improbable apotheosis, reunited with the man who came to
symbolize the purest Revolution, the most rigorous virtue,
the most exacting love—Brutus. As early as 1790, Voltaire's
play had been received with cheers; in spite of the disturbances provoked by the royalist factions who on some eve-
nings tried to drown out the play, it was a triumph. People
thought it especially ingenious that the actors reproduced at
the end of the tragedy, in a *tableau vivant,* David's canvas

22. The first two acts are set in the city of Caen, declared to be in a state of
rebellion and under siege by the republican forces. Charlotte, the widow of
a husband killed for "the prince," exhorts the inhabitants to be brave. In the
course of the third act, we see her penetrate into the enemy camp and
assassinate Marat, who acknowledges all his crimes during a long monologue in which he invokes Saint-Just, Lebas, and David: "Toi dont
j'admirai le pinceau plein de feu, / Peindre l'horreur d'un Roi et le mépris
d'un Dieu." ["You whose fiery brush I admired, / Painting the horror of a
King and the contempt of a God."] At the end Charlotte marries the
liberator of the city.

entitled *La Mort de Titus*.[23] "Brutus" became fashionable as a nickname.[24] The decree of 2 August 1793, proposed by Couthon, enacted the following measure:

Starting on the fourth of this month, and until the first of September next, there shall be performed three times weekly, in the theaters of Paris that shall be designated by the municipality, the tragedies *Brutus, William Tell, Caïus Gracchus,* and other dramatic plays that retrace the glorious events of the Revolution and the virtues of the defenders of Liberty. One of these performances shall be given every week at the expense of the Republic.[25]

Brutus, "by and for the people," was presented in nine different theaters. It became so closely associated with the Revolution that one of the first tragedies of the reaction was entitled by its author, Calland, *Encore un Brutus ou le Tribunal Révolutionnaire de Nantes* [*Yet Another Brutus, or the Revolutionary Tribunal of Nantes*].[26] When, on 14 August 1793, one Sylvain Lejeune requested of the Convention that the public forges produce instruments of revenge against traitors to the country, that all frivolous entertainments be immediately closed, and that all theatrical performances be suspended, the deputy Charles Delacroix protested, exclaiming that there was "no one who on leaving a performance of *Brutus,* was not inclined to plunge a knife into the scoundrel who would enslave his country."[27]

Voltaire's *Brutus* was not only the play most often performed during the revolutionary period, it became a symbol of civic uprightness. What a deputy said of Marat could be

23. Jacques Hérissay, *Le Monde des théâtres pendant la Révolution* (Paris: Perrin, 1922), p. 140. See also the excellent analyses of Jean Starobinski on the works of David in 1789, *Les Emblèmes de la raison* (Paris: Flammarion, 1979), pp. 72–76.

24. Cf. Jauffret, *Le Théâtre révolutionnaire,* p. 269.

25. Hérissay, *Le Monde des théâtres pendant le Révolution,* p. 140.

26. Jauffret, *Le Théâtre révolutionnaire,* p. 269.

27. Marvin Carlson, *Le Théâtre de la Révolution française* (Paris: Gallimard, 1970), p. 165.

said of Brutus: he represented a kind of "maximum" of
patriotism beyond which one could not go, an extreme and
resolute image of devotion to the people. Even when Voltaire's other plays were censored, *Brutus* was never attacked.
Always popular, challenged only by the royalist groups that
still frequented the theaters in 1790, the tragedy contributed
a final element to the judicial and theatrical system that
enabled Marat, like a king, to become father of a people.

Brutus is the tragedy of paternity or, rather, paternities,
dual paternities in constant opposition, divided by love and
the law that constitutes them. Brutus, having driven the
tyrant from Rome, must face up to the treason of his own
son Titus, and he chooses to have him executed. It is a
choice, for one knows that the Senate would have been
more indulgent and that Titus's guilt is not absolutely established. The infanticide thus becomes the supreme evidence
of a sublime paternity. At the start of the play, royal paternity, which will form a strong contrast with civil paternity,
is put on trial. Tarquin is the wrongful father against whom
no judgment is warranted, a father who is guilty but inviolable:

> Est-ce à vous de prétendre au droit de le punir,
> Vous, nés tous ses sujets; vous faits pour obéir?
> Un fils ne s'arme point contre un coupable père;
> Il détourne les yeux, le plaint et le révère.
> Les droits des souverains sont-ils moins précieux?
> Nous sommes leurs enfants; leurs juges sont leurs dieux.
>
> (I, 2)

How can you claim the right to punish him? you who were all
born his subjects, who were put here to obey. A son does not take
up arms against an erring father; he averts his eyes, laments and
reveres him. Are the rights of sovereigns less precious? We are their
children; their judges are their gods.

Set against this monarchical form of paternity that transcends right is a double paternity: natural paternity and the
civic paternity that emanates from the Law and is identified

with it. "Du peuple romain, le Sénat est le Père" ["The Senate is the Father of the Roman people"], says Valerius (I, 2), and Brutus says to his son:

> Va, ce n'est qu'aux tyrans que tu dois ta colère;
> De l'Etat et de toi je sens que je suis père.
>
> (IV, 6)

Go now, you owe your wrath only to tyrants; I feel that I am father to the state and to you.

The plot against the Senate is quickly termed "parricide" (V, 2).

It should not be thought, however, that it was enough that the father be elected, hence chosen, recognized, accepted, for a valid paternity to be instituted. Actually, when Brutus is spoken of as the father of liberty or Marat as the father of the people, everyone is aware that these two figures are also two regicides, two usurpers, and that their paternity was built on a parricide. One father ousts the other. In this tragic sequence, royal and absolute paternity—murder or exile—legal and civil paternity, it seems that from the murder of the father there emerges another father, but the link is more complex. The true condition of paternity, the only one that transcends nature and the law while being recognized by them, is expressed—as one might anticipate—not with reference to the fallen father (in the regicide which would be the basis of the new regime of law), but with reference to the heir, the son who bows to this new image, for it is filiation that will determine the true nature of paternity. One of the first causes of Titus's rebellion against his father, we are told, is Brutus's refusal to make Titus the favored son, the exception that would make the child the heir. Here was the absolute limit of civil paternity (and at the same time what founded it): it could not engender a prince. Tullia sees the danger and protests:

> Il n'a point sur son front placé le diadème;
> Mais, sous un autre nom, n'est-il pas roi lui-même?
>
> (IV, 3)

He has not placed the diadem on his brow; but is he not a king by another name?

Brutus replies in the most tragic terms: it is because between the father and the son there stands an obstacle that must prevent a hereditary power from forming, and this obstacle is the law. The law that makes Brutus a father constitutes the interdiction that enables Titus to assert himself as Brutus's son. "He blindly loves his country and his father," Messala says of Titus, but Brutus firmly replies:

> Il le doit: mais surtout il doit aimer les lois;
> Il doit en être esclave, en porter tout le poids.
>
> (II, 4)

As he should; but above all he ought to love the laws; he should be their slave, he should bear their full weight.

This makes it easier to understand what *La Feuille du Salut Public* found wrong with Mathelin's play, where it is stated that every citizen has no other master but the law, while the critic asserts that Marat should have risen above the law, as the paternal status and the seriousness of the circumstances gave him warrant to do. The law is a line of demarcation between father and son. It marks a separation that makes possible this paradox: revolutionary paternity does not allow children. There can be a Father of the People, a king without a crown whom regicide has placed above the law, but the people have no father or master except the legislative body. Far from being Brutus's complement, the new father of the Roman people, Titus is the danger. Filiation is the rock on which civil paternity may come to grief, and the law condemns this king without a patrimony to an exhausting solitude. The hereditary power of the king, the very notion of an heir, carries an interdiction more appalling than parricide itself: the regicide that *confers* paternity *excludes* the engendering of a child. The transmission of power is not possible; nothing could express more forcefully or more despairingly that short-lived paternity which the Revolution saw in the darkest hours of the Terror.[28]

Brutus, the murderer of his own son, saves his title of Father of the Country. The Constituent Assembly had thus voted, before dissolving, that none of its members could be elected to the Legislative Assembly that was to succeed it. This need for discontinuity, this refusal of filiation, was closely linked to that double movement that sacrificed one father and proclaimed another, this one childless. The trial of Charlotte Corday was to produce nothing else but the repeated affirmation that she acted alone, on no one else's behalf, that her act was not the beginning of a filiation but the ineluctable end of a resolution. One can doubtless say of Brutus, Marat, and Corday that each got rid of a tyrant, but one can say as well that what ultimately unites these three figures is the absence of a legacy, the separation that the law brings about between them and their heirs.[29]

In an essay entitled "Perspective de la mort dans la tragédie," Guy Rosolato remarks:

In tragedy there is a sort of "chain," a succession, a genealogy of deaths, as it were: to a previous death there corresponds a subsequent death or *end.* . . . This relationship goes beyond (or falls short of) expiation, or punishment, allowing the link of *succession*

28. Lynn Hunt, in an unpublished essay on "The Rhetoric of Revolution in France," notices a complementary ideology: "The radicals," she writes, "rejected paternal authority. . . . Mother republic might have her children and even her masculine defenders, but *there was never a Father present.*"

29. Frank Bowman cites speeches comparing Marat to Jesus, which opens new perspectives on the rhetoric of the Son forsaken by the Father. Cf. *Le Christ romantique* (Geneva: Droz, 1973), pp. 62–67.

to be glimpsed, like a *"cast shadow"* (to use Freud's expression) which, by the law of retaliation of the ancient world, gives *violent* death a force of attraction that might explain a previous phenomenon of *mourning* and identification. But above all, a genealogy with its successions shows forth: *as if a first violent death broke the genealogical succession and it was necessary that another death occur in order to reestablish the genealogical line through logical compensation.*[30]

The Revolution, which brought representation and execution together on the stage, was unique in that death, hence the breaching of a genealogy, never permitted that another death reestablish the succession, because the very possibility of genealogy, the paternal function, was guaranteed only by the absence of filiation.

30. Guy Rosolato, *Essais sur le symbolique* (Paris: Gallimard, 1969), p. 187 (emphasis in the original).

5

The Actor Marat

As early as 1788, in the lists of grievances addressed to the Etats-Généraux, the actors protested against their exclusion from political and religious life:

> It needs to be pointed out to the states that it is absolutely unjust that in such an enlightened century there exists a decree anathematizing a group of citizens who often, by reason of their private virtues, and always through their abundant alms, have every right to the indulgence of the Holy Father; and that he will be implored to treat us like the buffoons (a class of actors well below our own) who furnish amusement to the city of Rome, and against whom, even in his domains, the Holy Father has never issued an excommunication.[1]

Another letter objects:

> It is still the case that an actor is never appointed to be a municipal official and, what is even more absurd, that they are never allowed to hold an office, positions which they are able to acquire as others do, since they can be bought for a price; and that certain companies, such as the lawyers, extend things further, expelling from their midst individuals who marry, not just an actress, but even the daughter or niece of an actor.[2]

In the Assembly debates of December 1789, Laya argued that far from being unworthy of public consideration, ac-

1. Quoted by Jacques Hérissay, *Le Monde des théâtres pendant la Révolution* (Paris: Perrin, 1922), p. 35.

2. Ibid., p. 36.

tors were "the instrument used by the moralists of a nation. They make us see our passions in the mirror of human life, in order to put us to shame, and our faults, so that we may correct them."[3] The actor's work, like the work of justice, was exemplary, so it was only proper to grant them the title of *citizen* together with all the privileges pertaining to that title. Abbé Maury took strong exception to such a notion, declaring eloquently that the actor, like the executioner, had a "vicious" profession. On 24 December 1789, Baumetz, who was to play a leading role in the great judicial reform of 1791, replied with a convincing defense: "I am not aware of any laws that have declared actors to be vile," he exclaimed. "They are stigmatized by prejudice and the prejudice that stigmatizes them is the child of superstition."[4] Mirabeau improvised a brief exhortation in favor of the actors, and the same day the Assembly passed a decree establishing that actors would benefit from all the rights of man and of the citizen.

This decree, which officially put an end to the civil and religious persecution suffered by actors since the Middle Ages, did not, however, manage to "reintegrate" the actor into the society that constituted his audience—so complex was the relationship that joined the actor and his character; so difficult, too, the gaze that, fixed on the stage, confused Marat and his representative. In the gesture that granted the actor his political and religious rights, there was also a kind of demystification: it implied the recognition that beneath the makeup the ordinary citizen was still there, that under the costume of illusion there remained a tangible reality. In fact, the theater as a phenomenon ought to be dissociated from the recent tradition that envelops the actor in a romantic halo and makes him the center of his activity. The social situation of the actor, which was for centuries on the fringes of society, might be compared to a view of the actor himself on the fringes of theatrical activity—a position less paradoxical than one might think.

3. Ibid., p. 37.   4. Ibid., p. 41.

In his speech of 23 December 1789, Abbé Maury anathematized the executioner and the actor in the same breath, yet
the Revolution went on to rehabilitate and honor both the
executioner and the actor. The historical conjuncture has
impressed Roger Caillois: "This promotion of the executioner corresponded to the downfall of the king. The former
was admitted into legality at the moment when the latter
was expelled from it." The text from which this remark is
drawn, *La Sociologie du bourreau,* contains many elements
that are pertinent to our study. Caillois offers the following
reflections concerning the death (2 February 1939) of the
executioner Anatole Deibler: "This man had severed the
heads of four hundred of his fellow men, and *every time
curiosity had turned toward the person executed,* never toward
the executioner. Regarding him there reigned a conspiracy
of silence, to say the least."[5] Clearly, what is said here could
easily be applied to a conventional description of the theatrical act insofar as, if the role is well "executed," the spectator's attention does not turn toward the actor but toward the
character he embodies. Is not the best actor precisely the one
whose personality is most apt to disappear beneath the role
he is playing? Although the criteria for theatrical "action,"
the "acting" of a play, have varied considerably—from real-
ism to extravagance, from melodrama to understatement—
it remains nevertheless true that the actor is usually judged
by the apparent ease with which he submerges himself in
the role he executes. But let us return to Caillois's text. The
situation of the executioner with respect to the law he appears briefly to represent is actually complex and quite
specific: "In one important respect he is outside the law: he is
left out of the conscription rolls." The personage partici-
pates in a unique social structure, however, and this brings
him near to the sovereign: "The executioner's office is in
practice hereditary. When one wants to evince the fatality
that hangs over their life, one shows them to be the sons,

5. This text appears in *Le Collège de sociologie,* texts presented by Denis
Hollier (Paris: Gallimard, 1979), pp. 396–420.

grandsons, and great-grandsons of executioners." Further on, Caillois writes:

> The executioner is in contact with both worlds. He gets his mandate from the law, but he is its lowliest servant, the closest to the dark, peripheral regions where the very ones he combats stir about and hide. He seems to emerge from a terrible zone and to obscure the light of order and legality. *One would think that the garment with which he covers himself in order to officiate were a disguise.* The Middle Ages did not allow him to reside inside the towns. His house was built in the outlying areas. . . . Everything connects the executioner to the non-assimilable part of the social body.[6]

One can see the extent to which, in this persistent link that joins the spectacle and punishment, the elements redouble and divide at the same time. In the metaphor that would make the execution stage into the space of the theater, the executioner assumes the figure of the actor as a person insofar as the same opprobrium excludes them from public life, and he assumes the figure of the actor as an actor insofar as, under his disguise, he keeps that ability to efface himself which enables the victim alone (who would then be the character of comedy or tragedy) to attract and hold the audience's attention. This actor, barely tolerated in the towns, who must make himself into the image of another in order to officiate, evokes in a disquieting and continuous manner the one by whom justice is done, who must confront looks of fear mixed with admiration. Caillois, moreover, considering that unique moment when the Revolution executed a king, a father, and gave his executioner the honors of citizenship, imagines a sort of accursed couple who briefly trace the boundaries of law and punishment:

> Together they ensure society's cohesion. One, bearing the scepter and the crown, draws to his person all the honors that are due

6. Emphasis mine.

the highest power; the other bears the weight of the sins that the exercise of authority entails, however just and moderate it may be. . . . The sovereign and the public executioner are in like manner brought nearer to the homogeneous mass of their fellow citizens and at the same time are violently separated from it.

Just as there could be no revolutionary justice if the spectator did not sanction by his presence the legality of the judicial action, the execution could not be carried out without that disquieting and secret figure who was as necessary to the spectacle as was his victim. Executioners and actors, both excommunicated, both outside the law for centuries, obtained public acceptance simultaneously.

Acting Marat

At the center of the paternal question as it was framed, on the one hand, by the judicial system that enabled the execution of the king, the Father of the People, and, on the other hand, by the theatrical system that brought the parricides Brutus, Marat, and Corday to the stage, there is, as we have seen, the question of filiation; indirectly, the question of creation may perhaps enter, but more specifically it is the problematic of inheritance and transmission. This aspect of the question is emphasized by the tragic, repetitious, tireless way that the majority of revolutionary plays articulate the question which interrupted Robespierre's last bit of writing: "In whose name?" What is theater, after all, if not the relentless showing forth—in a persistent, oppressive, liberating, and, at times, desperate manner—of that judicial formula par excellence, *in the name of*.

The actor who put on makeup in that summer of 1793, applying to his cheeks the pale color of Marat, wrapping his hair in the stained turban that signified the poverty and integrity of the People's Friend, spoke *in the name of*. The actress who put on, one after the other, the modest shawl of

Charlotte Corday and the slightly faded costume of Liberty, in the splendid unself-consciousness that allowed her that metamorphosis, presented herself *in the name of.* The actors who brought *Brutus* to a close by meticulously reproducing David's painting *La Mort de Titus* also spoke *in the name of.*

Let us consider for a moment this formula, *in the name of.* It is first of all the expression of an authority. I speak *in the name of:* I am invested with a certain power that guarantees me the right to speak. This right is not that of the sovereign, or at least the expression of it is not the same, for though the king is himself the subject of a delegation of divine authority, the formula by which he emphasizes it is different and may be used only by him: "I, by the grace of God." Contrary to that singular assertion of an absolute power, a large number of magistrates could act, decide, speak in the name of a particular authority. The judge who ordered an execution in the name of the king received from the latter the right to pronounce the sentence. The people's representative who voiced the demand for the king's death had received from the people the right to vote in their name. The actor who went on stage and declaimed: "Mon bras a des tyrans repoussé les efforts; / J'aurai vécu sans honte et mourrai sans remords" ["My arm has thwarted the efforts of the tyrants; I shall have lived without shame and shall die without remorse"],[7] recited—obviously—in the name of Camaille Saint-Aubin, who wrote those lines, in the name of the spectators, who enabled the spectacle to take place, and above all, in the name of Marat, whom he had the object of representing.

Yet, if the formula *in the name of* involved the transfer of an authority, it also implied that this authority resided elsewhere, in another. The judge could not sentence in his own name, the deputy use his personal authority, or the actor take the place of his character. Hence, to speak *in the name of* is to signify the absence of; it is to make clear that the right to

7. *L'Ami du peuple,* III, 3.

speak is borrowed from another who is absent, and that this right perpetually remains a conferred right. This is doubtless the peculiar glory and the fundamental alienation of the actor, that the discourse he utters in profusion rightfully belongs to another, that his presence on the stage comes about under the cover of another, and that his speech is always exercised in the name of another.

To the reversibility of the spectator into an actor, to the spectator's ever-present and always deferred desire to speak, there corresponds a "spokesman" who expresses himself as another. Diderot's spectator who goes home and retells the scene he has witnessed, who mimes the spectacle he has observed, reproduces this requirement of the spectacle: that one never speaks in his own name. Every identity, all authority, all expression is essentially a borrowing, a transfer, a delegation. This is the second facet of the system of communication brought into operation in the theater: the deferred desire of the spectator is addressed by the conferred speech of the actor; in all its forms, in its decor, its dialogue, its costumes, the theater speaks repetitiously *in the name of.*

The formula, insofar as it conveys authority, refers back to the first authority confronted, that of the father. To speak in the name of is to recall that the name of the father underlies the discourse to come and antecedes the commencement of speech. The most visible elements of representation are first manifested as the twofold figure of the law and the father. We have seen this delegation, this contested inheritance, traverse the sessions of the tribunal and the theater alike, altering for a time the precarious equilibrium of the spectacle and the judgment.

However, it was not so much the figure of the father that governed this astonishing profusion of spectacles organized like so many repressions. Nor was it the image of parricide that alone governed the reappraisal of executions, the assassination of Marat, or the setting-up of the regime of representation. Here the law was not the rule that stood between father and son, it was the break; it was not the balance scales but the blade. It was an equilibrium only because, like Solomon's justice but more rigorous, it was forever slaying the child one desired. What revolutionary law said, what it persistently expressed, was that there was no identity between the king and the judge, between the Father and the people, between the actor and the character, between the spectator and the protagonist. In these networks of deferred desire and affirmed representation, the law and the stage maintained in their structures a distance that was never traversed, a gap impossible to close. It is more understandable, then, that the most rigorous elements of theatrical false illusion were put into place on that same revolutionary stage: the importance of the author's name printed on the playbill, the persistence of the actor under the mask of the character, the deliberate artificiality of dramatic writing and staging. As constraining as they were, these indexes nevertheless permitted a strangely isolated, floating factor that enabled the theatrical representation to convey, in its arbitrary manner, a force more consequential than the dramatic reality it had taken upon itself, in that year of 1793, to interpret.

Artaud wrote that "the image of a crime presented in the requisite theatrical conditions is something infinitely more terrible for the spirit than that same crime when actually committed."[8] Doubtless Artaud regarded the theater as being—within a reality that was itself rarely given as accessible or fully established—an illusion more unsettling and more dangerous than the perception, problematical or not, of that reality. Considered in this manner, the theater gathers into an irremediable fusion everything that everyday life already contains in the way of cruelty and profound perversity. This ability of the theater to catch hold—in, it should be added, a rather mysterious way—of the strangeness of the real was to give it its tremendous persuasive force.

8. Antonin Artaud, *The Theater and Its Double,* trans. Mary Caroline Richards (New York: Grove Press, 1958), p. 85.

In its two scenes, the theater and the tribunal—so close, and so dramatically reflective of one another—the Revolution underwent a kind of laceration. But who could claim, on reading the newspapers of the period, and viewing a pitiless system of justice in retrospect, that the representation of Marat's death offered to the spectator's imagination a more gripping image than the daily executions he could attend free of charge? Can one suppose that the verdict of guilt, i.e., death within twenty-four hours, could inspire less fear than the stage vision of a volcano engulfing the last of the sovereigns in its flames?[9] But this is a poor way to state the problem, for it privileges actual experience as the only valid model for representation. *Représentation*: the word is full of ambiguity. The English language always speaks of the "production" of a theater play, a more appropriate term which stresses the fact that the scene is never situated in relation to a pre-existing reality implicitly recognized as privileged. Even when it was representing Marat's death, we have seen how little the theater concerned itself with what became "history," or, rather, how theater constantly shunted history aside, preferring a distant clamor, with its barely formulated resistances, its half-manifest vehemence, to factual representation.

One must not think of "the requisite theatrical conditions" as being, in the staging of a play, what would be most apt to strike the imagination of a receptive spectator, but, on the contrary, what would be most apt to reveal that "this is theater." The very specificity of the theater lies in the way it maintains violence and alienation in a forever unresolved tension: the deferred desire of the spectator, the conferred authority of the actor—the spectacle is a borrowing, hence always a debt to be settled. Whatever manifests this characteristic constraint under the apparent illusion of the mask,

9. This is the way Sylvain Marechal's play, *Le Jugement dernier des rois,* ends. The special effects enjoyed considerable success.

the triviality of the illusion, is therefore apt to awaken in the audience—beyond the abiding desire to take the stage and speak—the immediate anxiety that knows that this speech has always already been delegated.

Criticism has long regarded the function of repetition as the defining characteristic of the theatrical endeavor, or at least as a function that determines it in its most visible and at the same time most profound manifestations: that is, the vision of the same text, played by the same actors, day after day, evening after evening, and with those repeated re-presentations, the promise of an eternal return. One remembers how Camus saw in the actor, as in Don Juan, the man of multiple existences, the hero without hope whose spirit is never pacified. Villiers de l'Isle Adam made the theater the setting of *L'Eve future,* and Jules Verne made it the locus of a disturbing ritual, recreated in the *Chateau des Carpathes.* [10] In point of fact, this is a strictly romantic perspective; further, it is a spectator's view of the actor. Only the spectator, with his desire for a reversibility, can conceive of this repetition as an ever-vital speech, an ever-possible life, a continually postponed death; after all, didn't Molière wait till the *end* of *Le Malade imaginaire* to die? But actors know very well that the theater is not, cannot be repetition; for the spectacle is a unique production, never entirely foreseeable and impossible to repeat with exactness. The theater happens only once. Is the text identical when a voice, sometimes the same, sometimes a different one, takes it up again, before a different audience, with intonations that are bound to vary, however imperceptibly? To imagine that the death of Marat on the stage is the reiteration of a pre-existing text is both to

10. This theme of the actor finding the stage to be a place of rebirth is a characteristically romantic one. This actor nearly always has in front of him, but hidden in semi-darkness, an ardent spectator, obsessed by the spectacle. In Jules Verne's text, La Stilla's admirer invents a device able to reproduce her image and her superb voice; in this way he attends a new performance every evening in his castle. The singer is dead, but the spectacle is miraculously preserved.

anticipate the event and to enclose it in a retrospective vision that oversimplifies it. Everyone knows of the superstition that says that if the dress rehearsal is perfect the first performance will not be successful, but that if the dress rehearsal is difficult the first performance will receive an ovation. From one spectacle to another, everything is dissolved and recreated. In the apparent succession of its performances, the theater is rupture and discontinuity. Imagine that faithful and enthusiastic spectator who, as in the texts of Hoffman and Jules Verne, every evening leans from the same balcony of the same theater, enthralled by that singer whose performances never exhaust her talent and her charm; is he not aware that every evening is like the first time? What justifies his renewed presence is that the spectacle he contemplates is always diverse, uneasy in its resemblance to the spectacle of the previous evening, and yet incomparably different. Artaud put this forcefully:

> All words, once spoken, are dead and function only at the moment when they are uttered . . . a form, once it has served, cannot be used again and asks only to be replaced by another, and . . . the theater is the only place in the world where a gesture, once made, can never be made the same way twice.[11]

The actor playing Danton, for example, who is about to recite a text, reply to other actors in front of a particular audience, and in a few moments cross the space that separates the wings from the stage, the darkness from the light, in order to declaim: "Citoyens, cette enceinte / Du sceau sacré des lois porte l'auguste empreinte" ["Citizens, this chamber bears the stamp of the sacred seal of the laws"], that actor who in a single phrase describes the judicial site and the theatrical site: whom is he addressing? Who are these citizens thus called upon? If he, an actor, speaks in the name of Danton, to whom is his utterance directed? To the

11. Artaud, *The Theater and Its Double*, p. 75.

other characters, of course, linked as he is by the seal of the spectacle, by the enclosed space, the costumes, the lights, the visibility, by the text that enjoins them to speak, to be silent, to listen, to reply; and to the spectators, certainly, the patriotic "citizens" with whom the audience must identify. We know, however, that the spectator no more identifies himself with the actor than with the audience he addresses; we know that the spectator, by virtue of a deferred desire for a substitution, accepts for a limited time a passivity that is never an acquiescence or a credulity.

It is evident that the implicit spectator and the spectator actually present are different in that petition without reply of the actor Danton. But if that other spectator is physically absent from the theatrical event, the need for him is no less great. As a matter of fact, for the theatrical illusion to be maintained it is not enough that the spectator who is actually present feign credulity. The actor speaking must not only hold forth in the name of a borrowed authority, he must also imagine a listener who, in the name of the spectacle, likewise enters into the strange display of unfolding illusion—a listener for whom the discernible difference between the actor and the character cannot be recognized as such; a spectator for whom the stage and the world merge together in a poignant in-difference and a certitude that is never shaken; a spectator who is not a victim of a well-organized resemblance, but who recognizes in the make-believe his only reality. Thus there emerges, listening to the actor Marat, that tenuous and necessary phantom between the actor and his audience: an imaginary gaze, attentive and captivated, silent and collusive, an intense spirit that *recognizes* the assassinated People's Representative, that *hears* his last words, that *sees* him come to life again—not a visionary, but the only being for whom same and other are eternally merged into one, for whom signs compel things, identities fuse together, appearances remain elusive and yet are accepted. The irrational thus haunts the wings, for who but the madman can in all certainty merge illusion and reality?

Who else can effortlessly ignore the *mise en scène* and see Marat stabbed by Charlotte Corday with ever-innocent eyes?

The implicit spectator is, then, the madman. The person addressed by the actor Marat, the actor Danton, is the one who drifts at the outer limits of reason, in that clear and empty space where similarities and signs make game of things and significations. Thus it is not surprising that the theater, like madness, became the object of a closure, a distancing and an internment at the same time. Between the actor and the executioner a kind of complicity was established, joining those two figures who must dematerialize before the inexorable or dreadful nature of the thing they have to accomplish. Their acts require their anonymity; their ceremony demands that they bow, disappear, before the gravity or the mystery of the spectacle in which they participate. However, once the actor comes on stage, that is, once the disappearance has been achieved, once the character's identity has been assumed, it is no longer the executioner's image that accompanies the actor but that of an urgent madness which is summoned up on the very stage of the theater. Is it any wonder that Peter Weiss paid a last homage to Marat by situating the representation of his death in an asylum, by imagining the inmates of Charenton as actors? The hospital, the suburbs, the prisons, where we know the theater had a special place under the Terror—the whole space of the spectacle emphatically signaled a steady displacement which recalled that to perform a play, to act a drama, is to solicit an irrational spectator, to call up madness itself.

Thus the strange ceremonial unfolds. The attentive spectator imagines, while watching the actor, a different self playing the role—in other words, he projects himself as an actor—and the player, apparently addressing the crowd massed around the stage, speaks to that imaginary madman whom he needs in order for the authority that has been delegated to him to be fully exercised at last. The "hypnotized" spectator envisaged by Artaud, that audience "in a trance," beleaguered by a deafening spectacle, was the possibility of madness confined in a limited space. One must go back to those pages of Artaud dictated by the passion for a theater perceived as inescapable dementia: "A kind of terror seizes us at the thought of these mechanized beings, whose joys and griefs seem not their own but at the service of age-old rites, as if they were dictated by superior intelligences."[12] For indeed the theater is at the same time that total divorce between the actor and the character, and the impossible soliciting of an audience prey to "the most mysterious alterations." Artaud's entire work on the theater is haunted by that latent need for a demented spectator, the distrust of a language that is the conveyer of order and reason, a theater that is "the double of another reality," the "ineffable anguish" of an audience "trapped in the theater as if in a whirlwind of superior forces."

We know that Artaud envisioned in the theater of cruelty a spectacle with the audience at its center:

> We abolish the stage and the auditorium and replace them by a single site, without partition or barrier of any kind, which will become the theater of the action. A direct communication will be re-established between the spectator and the spectacle, between the actor and the spectator, from the fact that the spectator, placed in the middle of the action, is engulfed and physically affected by it. This envelopment results, in part, from the very configuration of the room itself.[13]

As we see here, Artaud's strategy consisted in reducing to a minimum the problematical distance between the actor and the spectator and in integrating the spectator into the theatrical action in an almost spontaneous fashion, by placing him in the space once occupied by the players, as, for example, in a circus. This integration has its price. The credulous,

12. Ibid., p. 58.   13. Ibid., p. 96.

captivated, terrified, exalted spectator, surrounded on all sides by a strangeness that for him is real—this spectator is mad, of course, even if his is only that transitory madness which turns illusion into life itself. One can thus postulate that for Artaud the space of the theatrical stage was a metaphorical apprehension of his own madness, that the madman solicited by the actor would be beset from all sides, hence enclosed in his own divagations and in a sense neutralized from the moment that the theatrical gesture demands his presence. This estranged audience would be confined within the enclosure of the spectacle, which could not unfold without it.

There are chapters in the history of the theater that make its progress strangely similar to the history of madness: the expulsion from the nave, the excommunication of actors, an indeterminate wandering that did not allow most actors to settle anywhere, their presence being tolerated only for a few days at a time, as in those moments when carnival or the festival encouraged, and controlled, the mixing of heterogeneous beings and signs, when teratology became the measure of things. After this vagabond life came confinement in the theater, with its enclosed stage, its floor, its walls. Protected, censored, directed, the actors came to depend on the king, yet the king himself could not ensure that the church would grant them a Christian burial. Another failure of the Father of the People, of the protector whose gesture of clemency afforded no protection from funerary banishment.

By thus comparing theater and madness as double manifestations of an ancient prejudice that required a rational separation between the stage and the audience, between the actor and the citizen, while letting itself be fascinated by the tireless repetition of the allurement, we do, however, risk oversimplifying, reducing the theatrical phenomenon to summary oppositions. Similarly, to identify the implicit spectator as a *"spectataire"* (which one is tempted to do simply for the sake of convenience, following the example of the *narrataire* without whom the narration could not exist), would risk deflecting the theater away from its specificity. This implicit spectator is not necessitated by the theatrical text but only by the actor. He has no existence prior or subsequent to the spectacle; his troubled and credulous image, which duplicates the audience at the actor's first entrance, is obliterated at the moment the applause breaks out, finally giving the public the right to expression. He is the listener of a moment, the visionary of a brief glare, the shadow of an arranged and precarious simulacrum. His existence, in other words, is required only in terms of the actor. He does not double the audience, he complements the reciter; and it is not the least of the paradoxes on acting that the actor is forever giving rise to a personage about whom it is generally said that "he is not responsible for his actions."

We could thus conceive of the theoretical network outlined at the beginning of this essay (p. 12) as a circle. This network was presented as a sequence, not necessarily causal or diachronic in nature, but an organization where the resemblances laced together the elements of an insistent continuity between the tribunal and the theater. With their underlying symbolics of acknowledged paternity and impossible inheritance, we know that the two *scènes* exchanged their inherent discontinuity. The circle would not signify continuity, but contiguity. This contiguity is always on the verge of yielding to substitution: the trial of Louis XVI unfolded like a joyful and effervescent theatrical performance; Marat's death on the stage took on a gravity one would normally expect only at executions.

The displacements are no doubt discernible, but not where one would expect them to appear. Between these elements there is a circulation not so much of similarities as of borrowings. Trying the king not only required a new formulation of the law that would condemn the accused in advance, it demanded of another *scène* its rows of seats, its audience, its décor, its declamations, and the urgency of tragedy. Conversely, the theater borrowed more than the visible form of the trial from a juridical system drawn up with a view to the possible death of the Father of the People. Through the death of the king, the theater declared the rebirth of Marat: through Marat's public confession, it declared the carrying-out of an execution that would preserve the memory of Charlotte Corday next to Brutus in the hearts of citizens. What the judicial system and the theater shared as well was the practice of a violence exerted not where it ought to have manifested itself, that is, against the accused who appeared before his judges, but in a more insidious and oppressive manner, against those who silently watched the punishment they had demanded in delegating their own powers.

Hence the network suggests borrowing, debt, silence, oppression, and, at the outer edges of the scenic configuration, that imaginary spectator who would legitimate the illusion and accept that authority always emanates from the one who takes the floor and speaks. That "shadow figure" solicited by the actor should have been in a position to separate the stage and the tribunal in a decisive way. This was not the case, however, because he stood in for another hypothetical figure without whom the trial of Louis XVI could not have taken place. What in fact founded the new conception of revolutionary law was the people, but we know that the people could not take the place of the king, that is, they could not put themselves above the law that was to govern their acts and their functions. To formulate a system in the name of the people was to invoke an *impossible* people—at the same time above the law, since they founded it, and the object of that law, insofar as they were liable to suffer all its rigor. Writes François Furet:

From the spring of '89 onward, authority lost every anchoring point; it was no longer in any institution. . . . The Revolution was characterized by a situation in which authority was manifested as vacant; intellectually and practically, it had become free. . . . Speech replaced authority as the sole guarantee that power would only belong to the people, which is to say, to no one in particular. . . . In this collective delirium concerning authority, which henceforth governed the political battles of the Revolution, representation was excluded or constantly watched over.[14]

The power of the people or, rather, the people in possession of the power to found the law is, in a certain sense, the paradox inherent in saying *in the name of* while suggesting simultaneously that authority originates in the one who makes the statement.

Both Marat's death and the judicial complexity that made the king's execution possible structure the contiguous stages of the scaffold and the theater. This brief approach cannot account for all the dynamisms inherent in the theatrical function nor can it account for the notion of "revolutionary theater." Moreover, the critical function is too closely tied to the situation of the spectator to aim here to go beyond a particular field of view: 1793; Plancher-Valcour has already torn away the veil of the Délassements-Comiques theater; the lights have just gone down, plunging the audience into semi-darkness and calling for silence; the commotion has not completely subsided, but the actor is ready to speak. He wears the turban of Marat, his costume reveals his poverty, he has a quill pen in his hand—as you see, this is a preamble.

14. François Furet, *Penser la Révolution française* (Paris: Gallimard, 1979), pp. 71–72.

Designer: Marion O'Brien
Compositor: Innovative Media, Inc.
Printer: Thomson-Shore, Inc.
Binder: John H. Dekker & Sons, Inc.
Text: 10/12 Bembo
Display: Bembo Italic